The White Burkett
of Public A
at the University

# Problems and Prospects of Presidential Leadership in the Nineteen-Eighties

VOLUME II

James Sterling Young
Editor

UNIVERSITY
PRESS OF
AMERICA

LANHAM • NEW YORK • LONDON

Copyright © 1983 by

**University Press of America,™ Inc.**

4720 Boston Way
Lanham, MD 20706

3 Henrietta Street
London WC2E 8LU England

**Library of Congress Cataloging in Publication Data**
(Revised for volume 2)
Main entry under title:

Problems and prospects of presidential leadership in the
    nineteen-eighties.

    At head of title: The White Burkett Miller Center of
Public Affairs at the University of Virginia.
    Essays from a series of four roundtable discussions held
1979-1980 at the Miller Center of Public Affairs,
Charlottesville, Va.
    Includes bibliographical references.
    1. Presidents—United States—Addresses, essays,
lectures. 2. United States—Politics and government—
1945-        —Addresses, essays, lectures. I. Young,
James Sterling. II. White Burkett Miller Center.

JK516.P76   1982        353.03'1          82-19981
ISBN: 0-8191-2908-9 (pbk.: v. 2)
ISBN: 0-8191-2907-0 (v.2)

# FOREWORD

The purpose of the Miller Center, mandated in part by its founder, Burkett Miller, is to further the understanding and improvement of the presidency. The joint National Academy of Public Administration-Miller Center project on the changing milieu of presidential leadership is particularly well suited to further both dimensions of the Center's mission. Students and citizens can draw on the essays of the major contributors in this volume to enhance understanding. Public servants and elected officials may discover new approaches to the improvement of government and more particularly the presidency. Some of the nation's foremost presidential scholars and interpreters met in Charlottesville in 1979-80. Freed from the pressures of Washington, New York and other large urban centers, they devoted themselves uninterruptedly to a series of roundtable discussions. The Council and staff of the Miller Center were especially pleased to make available the historic setting of Faulkner House for serious discourse on some fundamental problems of the presidency.

*Kenneth W. Thompson*
*Director, White Burkett Miller*
*Center of Public Affairs*

# EDITOR'S PREFACE

The essays in this volume grew out of a series of roundtable discussions at the Miller Center of Public Affairs on the general subject of the changing milieu of presidential leadership and its implications for the presidency in the decade ahead. Held in 1979-1980 at the Center's Faulkner House in Charlottesville, these roundtables—four in all—focused, respectively, on the emergent political setting of the presidency, the institutional setting, the congressional setting, and the international setting. The conferees included academicians, present and former members of Congress and other public officials, Washington journalists, and members of private consulting firms.

At each of the roundtables political scientists were asked to serve as discussion leaders, offering their perspectives and insights on the subject at hand for group discussion. From their oral presentations these scholars subsequently prepared essays for publication under the sponsorship of the Miller Center. The authors of the essays in this volume were the discussion leaders at the second roundtable where the subject was the changing character of the Congress and its implications for presidential leadership. Volume I in the series contains essays on the political and institutional settings for the presidency in the nineteen-eighties; Volume III deals with the international environment.

All three volumes share a common purpose. They trace the changes in the American political system that have occurred in the last fifteen years, and assess the cumulative impact of these changes on the future of the presidency and its role of political leadership in the American polity and in the society of nations.

That there has been a resurgence of congressional power in recent times is well recognized. Symbolized in the impeachment moves against President Nixon, this resurgency has been evidenced in wide-ranging congressional actions restrictive of presidential power and prerogative: actions that recall loans of legislative authority extended to the presidency in earlier times; actions that attach new conditions to presidential use of delegated authority; interdictions of presidential actions through the assertion of the legislative veto; new forms of legislative oversight of both presidential conduct and executive branch programs.

Less well publicized, but perhaps more enduring and more consequential in their implications for the presidency, have been changes within Congress itself that have attended the resurgence of its power. These are the changes that are explored in this volume.

In the first essay, Thomas E. Mann examines the external forces that may be bringing about changes in the kinds of people who seek legislative seats, win them, and succeed in keeping them: new sources and methods of campaign funding; new methods and styles of campaigning; new interest group organizations; changing national demographics. His essay points out how these changes, all beyond presidential control, may affect both the composition of Congress and the strategies of influence pursued within it in ways having major impact on congressional disposition to follow the White House lead.

Norman J. Ornstein, in his essay, reviews the internal reforms enacted by Congress and by the congressional party organizations in recent years, particularly those affecting the role and power of the congressional party leadership. Pointing out that a process of democratization inside Congress has attended the resurgence of congressional power vis-a-vis the President, Mr. Ornstein notes the resulting dilemmas for those who would attempt to lead Congress either from within or from the White House; and he suggests some guidelines for leadership strategy that would at the least avoid the exacerbation of those dilemmas.

With the phenomenal growth in congressional staff during the last fifteen years, an institutionalized presidency now confronts an institutionalized Congress, staffed up ostensibly to support its exercise of new power. Allen Schick's essay probes beneath the surface of this development to scrutinize the nature, impact, and unwritten functions served by congressional staff growth. Among other conclusions of pointed consequence for presidential leadership, his essay suggests that this development has elevated the real influence of nonelected echelons in an elected body, has equipped individual legislators to act independently of party or presidential leadership, and has encouraged them to take active roles in areas of policy where their own personal interest or expertise may be slight.

In the concluding essay Harvey C. Mansfield, Sr. considers how changes in Congress are likely to affect interactions between the executive and legislative branches. Reviewing trends in presidential-congressional relations, Mr. Mansfield sees little prospect of a return to old-style congressional oligarchies or to the kind of license for presidential leadership that Roosevelt enjoyed, and little prospect, either, for constitutional reform to overcome the difficulties of an inescapably overburdened presidency and an assertive, generously staffed, politically fragmented Congress. His essay offers a prognosis of muddling through the nineteen-eighties. Indeed it suggests that there may be some virtues in that sort of traditional method of coping with the problems of governance in a system of separated institutions sharing powers.

*James Sterling Young*

# ACKNOWLEDGEMENTS

For co-sponsorship of the roundtable series for which earlier versions of the essays in this volume were prepared, the Miller Center acknowledges with gratitude the National Academy of Public Administration. Among other purposes, the roundtable discussions were intended as background for the Academy's Panel on Presidential Management and to supplement the research studies of the Panel's staff. The Panel's report and recommendations have been published by the National Academy under the title *A Presidency for the 1980s* (Washington: National Academy of Public Administration, 1980). Research studies prepared by the panel's staff have been published under the title *The Illusion of Presidential Government*, edited by Hugh Heclo and Lester M. Salamon (Boulder, Colorado: Westview Press, 1981).

The Miller Center gratefully acknowledges also the support of Mr. Sydney Stein, Jr.

Messrs. David Clinton and Robert Strong helped in many crucial ways with both the organization and administration of the roundtable series. Ms. Anne Quigley provided valuable editorial assistance in preparing this volume. To them and to the staff of the Miller Center, special thanks is here expressed.

# CONTENTS

# CHANGES IN THE EXTERNAL POLITICAL ENVIRONMENT OF CONGRESS:
## Implications for Congressional Leadership

Thomas E. Mann
*Adjunct Scholar*
*American Enterprise Institute*
*Executive Director*
*American Political Science Association*

My purpose in this essay is to explore these questions: What changes are taking place in the external political environment in which legislators get nominated, elected and lobbied by constituents and other groups—particularly those changes that can be expected to affect their political behavior in Washington in relation to the President and the executive branch? What kinds of problems, opportunities, and demands are these trends likely to pose for Chief Executives serving in the 1980s?

Separating the external environment from internal processes is no easy task. To understand how Congress changed in the 1970s, one must explore how developments outside Congress— massive membership turnover in both House and Senate, the recruitment of new-style candidates, changes in the conduct of campaigns and in the structure of competition—interacted with changes that were occurring within the institution. In the course of this essay, I will perforce shift back and forth between the environment and the institution, although my focus clearly is on the former.

One danger in concentrating on change is that we may easily overemphasize the importance of recent developments while ignoring stable elements that determine the basic shape of the political process. I have in mind here several enduring characteristics of our political system that together work against central authority. First, of course, is our Madisonian system with its constitutional separation of the executive and legislative branches. The indepen-

1

dent electoral bases of the president and Congress virtually ensure a degree of institutional tension not seen in parliamentary systems. Second, the United States has always had a unique political party system, one that is highly decentralized, factionalized and personalistic, with relatively little programmatic coherence. American parties have never been strong in a European sense; and even when certain local party organizations were robust, it didn't necessarily strengthen the hand of the president. It's easy to slip into a discussion of the good old days of strong parties that in fact never existed in American politics. Third, since the late 19th Century, the Congress has exhibited a high level of professionalism, with a relatively stable membership that has an obvious interest in preserving and enhancing long-term political careers. Voluntary retirements from the Congress increased during the 1970s, but perhaps more important is the continuing desire of most senators and representatives to remain in office and to develop politically and personally rewarding legislative careers. This also works to exacerbate institutional tensions. Fourth, activist Democratic presidents since the 1930s have faced the formidable opposition of the conservative coalition in Congress. While there has been a certain ebb and flow to the coalition, and the changing political complexion of the South has probably weakened it, the coalition continues to pose a problem for Democratic presidents with ambitious legislative proposals in the areas of civil rights, social welfare and foreign policy.

Quite apart from any recent changes, then, American politics in the normal course of events is biased against decisive executive leadership, especially in domestic policy-making. Only on occasion have events and political forces combined to produce intense cooperation between the president and Congress; those bursts of legislative activity have seldom been sustained beyond a couple of years.

There is another potential danger in focusing all of our attention on recent changes in the external environment: many of the lessons of the past two decades may be reversed in the 1980s. To jump ahead of my argument for a moment: while in the 1970s we saw a seemingly permanent Democratic majority in the Congress, an enhanced advantage of incumbency (especially in the House), and a dominance of local candidates over national issues and parties in congressional elections, the 1980s may bring Republican control to one or both houses, the rise of serious challengers in many House as well as Senate races, and a heightened attention by individual voters to the record and the image of the two parties. Trends set in motion in the past need not continue predictably into the future. We need to be aware of these possibilities and strive to understand what the institutional consequences of further changes in the external environment would be.

One final note of caution. Whatever the structural characteristics of its environment, Congress retains the capacity to change direction in response to major shifts in public opinion. Congress is a representative institution and, on matters of pressing national concern, a reactive institution. A crisis or a newly emergent national consensus can lead Congress to act expeditiously (even precipitously), contrary to what we might have otherwise predicted. Policy reversals are not characteristic of the American political system, but they are possible.

With these qualifications, I now proceed to discuss recent changes in the way members are nominated, elected, and lobbied and to explore the implications of these changes for presidential leadership.

### Nomination

I take issue with scholars who have argued that in recent years there has been an enormous diminution in the influence of party in the nomination of members of Congress. The most significant change in the nomination process took place in the beginning of this century with the adoption of the direct primary; since that time the stability in the methods of nomination has been more important than the change. Congressional candidates in years past were usually self-selected. They had to put together their own political organizations in seeking the nomination; the role of party has always been relatively weak. And even with the urban machines where party officials typically hand-picked congressmen, the interests were predominantly local; only occasionally did they coincide with what might be on the agenda of the national party.

To be sure, nomination politics were somewhat more structured in the past. There was a time when there were "elders" in the district, who looked for the best candidate and mobilized their resources to move that candidate forward. That is, there were a limited number of major interests that someone had to deal with in getting the nomination. The growing political mobilization and political organization of diverse groups in districts has led to many more opportunities for individuals operating outside those major interests. That's partly a result of changes in the conduct of campaigns, especially in the use of the media. Different types of individuals are attracted to these more fluid situations, and they may behave differently in office than those recruited in more structured settings.

Nelson Polsby has made an argument very much along these lines. As recent as the 1950s, he speculates, more than half of all congressmen came from districts with significant party organizations, be they large urban machines, the Democratic courthouse rings or their Republican counterparts in the Northeast and Midwest. The contrast in legislative style between these party-initiated members (or party regulars) and the self-starters was striking, as Leo Snowiss demonstrated in his study of Chicago-area congressmen. Party regulars were likely to be followers and compromisers while the self-starters tended to be more issue-oriented and publicity-conscious. Over the last two decades, the proportion of members elected from districts with some substantial party presence in the nominating process has probably declined to a third or less, meaning the mix in Congress has been altered to include more new-style members with very individualistic perspectives on their careers. While this is a significant development, it is very clearly not an abrupt break with the past.

One important aspect of continuity in the nomination process is the fact that incumbents seldom face serious primary opposition. Many years ago, V. O. Key reported that primary elections in the South were no substitute for two-party competition. It's pretty much the same story nowadays. This doesn't mean that members of Congress are free from worry about primaries. Every election year some incumbents are denied renomination, and the lessons of the few are shared by the many. Moreover, the political importance of primary defeats often outweighs their number. For example, ten committee chairmen in the House of Representatives were defeated in primary elections between 1964 and 1972. The general point here, in thinking about signals being sent to members and the lessons learned from the experience of getting nominated and renominated, is that basically they are on their own. With a direct primary, incumbents need to discourage serious opposition. The local party is sometimes a force to be reckoned

4

with; it's more important in some districts than in others. Candidates are political entrepreneurs in seeking and retaining their nomination, and their political party has relatively little to do with it.

A second point about nominations is that the 1980s may see a move in the direction of a more assertive role for the national parties in the nomination process. Traditionally, the national party organizations have stayed clear of local contests for nominations, realizing they would have to live with whomever was elected. Yet in recent times the national Republican party has abandoned its reticence in this regard—at least temporarily. Under the leadership of Republican National Committee chairman Bill Brock, the GOP has taken the lead in encouraging strong candidates to run, in providing financial and technical assistance to candidates, in developing a more attractive party image, and in planning a recruitment and apportionment strategy with respect to state legislators. Brock has recognized that the Republicans have had difficulty recruiting good candidates to run for Congress, and that they are in very bad shape with respect to the redistricting that will occur after the 1980 apportionment. So he has poured substantial resources into trying to turn both of those situations around by fielding good candidates for state legislative races and getting them elected. The early indications are that he's had some success; it is likely to continue in 1980. The state legislatures have always been the primary recruitment pool for Congress; anywhere from a third to a half of all members of Congress first serve in state legislatures. To the extent those state legislative races are visible, those candidates are one step up in mounting a congressional challenge.

Two caveats must be offered on the GOP strategy on the recruitment of candidates. First, however imaginative and vigorous their efforts, the Republicans will find that most of the action is beyond their control or influence. As Gary Jacobson and Samuel Kernell have persuasively argued, potential candidates and contributors make their own rational calculations about whether to run or whether to help underwrite a challenge based largely on their perceptions of the likelihood of success. National political conditions—particularly the popularity of the president and the state of the economy—figure prominently in their calculations. If, as in 1980, the climate favors the Republicans, good GOP candidates will come forward, whatever the efforts of the national party.

Conversely, if, as in 1974, national conditions are working against the Republicans, there is little the national party can do to persuade the strongest potential candidates to enter the race.

Second, organization and activity usually breed counter-organization and activity. While the national Democratic party has lagged far behind the GOP in the area of congressional candidate recruitment and assistance, eventually they are likely to pursue the same kind of strategy, offsetting what is now a Republican advantage. I do not mean to suggest that nomination politics will lose its traditional local cast, only that to the extent there is any change in what now occurs, it will be an intensification of national participation in that system.

I have already discussed the importance of the nomination system for the type of individual recruited to Congress—and in turn for the legislative styles dominant within the institution. But other factors as well influence who seeks the nomination, and changes in these factors can account for important changes within Congress.

We have always had "period effects": people who run for office reflect the temper of the times. For example, that class of 1974 came in hard on the heels of Watergate; great emphasis was given to "cleaning up the process" and to financial disclosure. Many of these members were weaned politically on the anti-war movement; they were fundamentally anti-institution and highly issue-oriented. Obviously, there are exceptions, and any generalization one makes is vulnerable to the cases that don't fit. But as a rule, I think, this description fits the class of 1974. The class of 1978, on the other hand, is a very different breed. They're the Marty Sabos of Minnesota and the Bill Ratchfords of Connecticut, both former speakers of their state legislatures. These are people who are much less likely to be outsiders concerned with playing to a national and state press; they are institution types who believe in compromise and strong leadership, division of labor, and quietly working along. My impression is that legislative style is partly a function of times. And 1978 was very different from 1974. If Maguire and Moffett are representative in some way of the class of 1974, then Sabo and Ratchford are more representative of the class of 1978. We shouldn't generalize from what we saw happening in the mid-seventies to the eighties, because the next decade may see a very different breed of new member.

Another question in terms of recruitment is: do the modern conditions of campaigning discourage some types of individuals and encourage others? The people who were not dissuaded from seeking office by the new financial disclosure requirements were, for the most part, those who had nothing to disclose. They were often people fresh out of law school who worked for a public interest law firm, had relatively uncomplicated financial lives, took to the media very well, knew how to enlist volunteers and to raise money, and so on. At the same time, another type of candidate—one who after twenty years of successful business experience decided to run for Congress and serve his district for a period of years—might be discouraged by the way in which financial backgrounds are disclosed and by the nature of the media campaigns. The kind of person who comes to Congress is as important for understanding how the institution operates as the internal rules. What will be the values about government of those recruited to Congress in the 1980s? Will they value compromise? Will their incentives be defined internally or externally? The answer is not obvious. But if we want to know what's going to be occurring in Congress during the eighties, we have to know the kinds of people who are likely to be attracted to it.

One final point in this section concerns changes in the pattern of retirements. There was a substantial increase in retirements beginning in 1972 in both the House and the Senate, the causes of which have been discussed at length elsewhere. The job is much tougher, the life isn't as pleasant, the pace is excruciating, the rewards for longevity are greatly reduced, the financial benefits elsewhere are more substantial, and so on. Do we assume now that high turnover is the new norm? Or will we settle back into the pattern of modest retirements characteristic of the fifties and sixties? The early evidence is that in 1980 the number of retirements will be the lowest in over a decade. With a more stable membership, we may see a different kind of Congress, with certain changes made to strengthen its institutional capabilities. What would be the likely consequences if in the eighties electoral defeat replaced retirement as the primary source of turnover? Would partisanship increase? Would members become more or less individual entrepreneurs in their districts? Would the institution be strengthened or weakened? The answers are not obvious, but the questions deserve our serious consideration.

# IMPLICATIONS FOR PRESIDENTIAL LEADERSHIP

## *General Election*

While changes in the structure of general elections are more pronounced than in the nomination system, congressional elections today nonetheless look a lot like congressional elections of the past. Most House districts are Democratic or Republican seats; they are seldom taken over by the opposition party. This is changing somewhat. There are prominent examples of seats that had been safe for a Republican suddenly becoming safe for a Democrat, and vice versa. The argument is made that seats are no longer safe for parties, only for individuals. Yet, it's still true that most seats don't switch parties. Years ago, Charles Jones found that about thirty percent of all districts changed parties over the course of a decade, a figure not all that different from today. In the open seats in 1978, where no incumbent was running, less than a fourth changed party hands, even though these were deemed the most vulnerable to opposition party takeover.

The partisan mold of states is significantly less set than of districts. Many states regularly elect to the Senate both a Democrat and a Republican; the number of states doing is increasing. In 1959, for example, 14 states were represented by both a Democratic and Republican senator; by 1979, the number of states with a split partisan delegation to the Senate had increased to 26.

Another element of continuity is the fact that House incumbents who seek reelection almost always succeed—this has been true for many decades. Once again, the Senate is somewhat of an exception.

Finally, congressional elections are influenced by both local and national forces, but the former are dominant. This stands in sharp contrast to Britain, where the swing is very uniform across constituencies. Some years ago, Donald Stokes argued that this local character of U.S. congressional elections was changing, that there seemed to be a nationalization of political forces underway, making the U.S. more like the British system. In fact, recent evidence suggests that the 1960s and 1970s have seen a further localization in political forces. In any case, the observation that "all politics is local" has fit congressional elections for many years.

What changes have occurred in the way members get elected and reelected in the Congress?

1. *Decline in the competitiveness of elections.* While incumbents have

always had a high degree of success in seeking reelection, the margins of their victory increased significantly beginning in the mid-1960s. The number of districts that hovered around the 50-percent mark, highly vulnerable to strong national tides and to local challengers, declined markedly as new-style congressmen, utilizing the increasing resources of incumbency, extended their victory margins well beyond their natural partisan base. This "vanishing marginals" phenomenon, as David Mayhew called it, was concentrated in districts with relatively new incumbents running. Open seats remained as competitive as before, and veteran Congressmen amassed no special advantage beyond the partisan edge in their districts.

2. *Increase in the resources available to incumbents.* Incumbents now have more resources—available by virtue of their office—to present themselves to their constituents in a positive light and to control the communications that voters receive about them. These include increases in staff, the placement of staff in district offices, the use of the frank, casework demands and resources, funds for travel back home, access to the media, and so on. While senators and representatives have shared equally in the fruits of official Washington's generosity, these resources have a greater electoral payoff in the House than in the Senate, primarily because senators more than representatives face competing sources of publicity about their actions in Congress.

3. *Changes in the relative mix of national and local forces.* As I just suggested, there has been an important change in the relative mix of local and national forces. The amount of local variation in House elections tripled between 1958 and 1978, reflecting the fact that more and more of the changes in a district's returns from one election to the next are specific to the local candidates, issues and events, not to what's happening at the national level. The change has really been quite remarkable. Coupled with this increasing localization has been a continuing decline in the extent to which presidents and legislators have shared electoral fates. An essential part of the political dynamism in our system has always come from popular presidential candidates sweeping into office with them many new congressmen who, at least for a year, give them critical support on their major policy proposals. Because of the commanding attention given issues in local races, presidential and congressional electorates have now become so separate

that this is much less likely to happen. The contrast between LBJ's Democratic party victory in 1964 and Richard Nixon's personal triumph in 1972 is striking.

This is not to argue that national political forces have no influence on congressional races—the Republican losses in the 1974 elections had much to do with Watergate, the Nixon pardon and the recession. National conditions shape the overall results—which party gains and by how much—but they are of secondary importance in local races where the mix of candidates and campaigns influences many more votes.

4. *Decline in party-line voting in congressional elections.* There has been a decline in party-line voting in congressional elections (the number of party defectors doubled between 1958 and 1978) and a growing centrality of candidate evaluations. We used to think that the public didn't know anything about the candidates; we've revised that view, partly because we are in a better position to measure it, partly because there has been some real change. The public knows who their congressman is, they have a generalized image of him or her, they often know who the challenger is. Although their knowledge about the positions their congressman takes and the votes he casts is almost nonexistent, they do have a reasonably accurate picture of the general ideological stance of their member. These perceptions of the candidates and their relative attractiveness, not party identification, are the primary determinants of the vote.

5. *Decline in turnout.* In 1978, only 35.1% of the eligible electorate went to the polls. It may be that many of the recent changes in congressional elections can be traced to the dropping out of the electorate of certain categories of people. While there has been a decline in voting participation, other types of political participation have increased. The activists are more politically active while the voters stay home.

6. *Changes in the conduct of congressional campaigns.* Perhaps the most dramatic development in congressional elections has been in the nature of the campaign itself.

    a. *campaign finance*—Congressional campaigns are considerably more expensive now than in the past and the sources of funds and the techniques of fundraising have changed. Between 1972 and 1978 the total amount raised for campaigns increased 137 percent for the House and 183 percent for the Senate, both much higher than the inflation rate. Between 1974 and 1978 the average House campaign expenditure grew from $54,000 to $109,000, the average Senate expenditure from $437,000 to $971,000. But the figures were higher in those races that were seriously contested (roughly 30 percent of all House contests and 70 percent of all Senate contests). In 1978, for example, successful House challengers spent well over $200,000 each. The increased cost of campaigning combined with the restrictions imposed by federal legislation has dramatically altered the way in which funds are raised. National political action committees (PACs), direct mail solicitation and candidates' personal contributions have all become more important, while the role of parties and large contributors has diminished. (The national Republican Party may well reverse this trend, since they aspire in 1980 to contribute over $20 million to Republican congressional candidates.) More money is being raised outside congressional districts and states, and early contributions by national groups, are playing an increasingly important role in legitimizing local challengers. Finally, now in 1980, independent expenditures by political action committees are beginning to play a growing role in congressional campaigns.

b. *media emphasis*—Candidates are relying more upon the media, particularly television, radio and direct mail. Much of this is done by incumbents in their official capacity—the in-house media capacity of the Congress is well situated for continuous campaigning. The structure of the media market in some districts mitigates against reliance on television, but in these cases highly sophisticated direct mail techniques are available. Media advertising is very expensive but also essential for challengers striving to become known to the voters in their districts.

One interesting aspect of the utilization of media in the 1980 congressional elections is the $9 million national television advertising campaign launched by the Republican National Committee. The commercials are designed to heighten national attention to the record and image of the two parties, especially to the alleged failures of 25 years of Democratic control in Congress. Whether or not the commercials succeed in 1980, they may presage an

11

increasing amount of communication from the national parties during the next decade, which may counter the individualistic character of most campaigns.

c. *campaign consultants*–A telling sign to potential contributors of the viability of a particular candidate is whether the campaign has hired nationally recognized professional consultants. The use of outside consultants—for polling, media, targeting, fundraising and campaign management—has increased noticeably in recent years.

d. *personal organizations*—As local political party organizations have weakened, congressional candidates have substituted their own personal organizations often staffed with large numbers of volunteers. Even in areas where the party maintains some significant organizational presence, candidate organizations often take on a very separate existence.

e. *year-round campaigning by incumbents*—Most House elections are effectively over before the onset of the fall campaign, since in most districts a decision will have been made much earlier not to wage a serious challenge. Incumbents are better able to discourage potentially strong challengers and their contributors as a result of their continuous campaigning. Members of Congress have become very resourceful in devising ways of appearing before their constituents which stress their personal concern for and responsiveness to their constituents—town meetings, work days and mobile offices are representative of these devices. In addition, of course, members constantly communicate with their constituents through the mail, in the newspapers, and on radio and television. For new-style congressmen, campaigning never stops.

Congressmen carry away several lessons from the rigors of modern campaigning. Now, even more than in the past, they feel largely responsible for their own electoral fates. Members worry about adverse national conditions, particularly when their party controls the presidency, but they realize that they can't do much about them. The clearest way to cut their losses is not to try to make the President look better or the economy improve— their actions are deemed too marginal to make a difference—but instead to concentrate on their own personal reputations in their constituencies. And these reputations, they believe correctly, are largely independent of the performance of Congress as an institution.

In addition, members worry more about reelection than appears justified by objective measures of their electoral success. They have good reason to worry. Their investment—in personal energy, money and career choice—is very high, yet subject to immediate depreciation. Dramatic shifts in district returns are not uncommon, and members typically think in terms of a sequence of elections, not just the immediate one. Any sign of weakness is likely to attract more serious opposition next time, and the advantages of incumbency wane in the face of a well-known, well-financed opponent. The stories of those who lose are told and retold in the cloakrooms as members try to develop their own early warning systems. Senators have even more reason than representatives to learn the lessons of their fallen colleagues.

As a consequence, members invest considerable energy in seeking to forestall a strong challenge, by acting continuously to enhance their personal reputations and by coming to grips with the major interests that might underwrite such a challenge. The latter might entail simply writing off such interests because their views are so diametrically opposed; or it might involve reaching an accommodation. In either case, members are pulled inevitably into conversation and dealings with community leaders and activists on legislative matters that largely escape the attention of the rank-and-file voter.

### Lobbying by constituents and other groups

The explosion of the public *agenda* has dramatically increased the number of groups with a strong interest in decisions made in Washington. Many of these groups are very specialized—witness the much-heralded single issue politics—and exist only to influence public decisions. Partly as a consequence, the power of large national interests with multiple goals has declined.

This transformation of the public agenda has also elevated the political clout of the public sector and its nongovernmental shadow. While iron triangles—which involve cozy relationships among federal agencies, congressional committees and interest group clients—are decades old, on an increasing number of issues, political appointees, congressional staff, career civil servants, and private and nonprofit sector experts define the terms of debate for elected officials. These "issue networks" become more prominent as the scope and complexity of governmental programs increase. In addition, the massive flow of dollars to state and local governments has led to a formidable intergovernmental or public sector lobby in Washington, increasing the particularistic tendencies in Congress.

Interest groups have become increasingly sophisticated in an organizational sense, combining grass roots lobbying with a Washington presence. The capacity of groups to stimulate communications from their members in constituencies across the country has been strengthened, and senators and representatives understandably find it worth their while to listen to these messages from back home, which are often more persuasive than entreaties from national lobbyists.

Groups have also been more inclined to adopt electoral strategies, involving efforts both to deliver group resources to candidates (money or volunteers, for example) and to influence public opinion (the environmental movement's "dirty dozen" and the 1980 independent television campaign against several Senate liberals by the National Conservative Political Action Committee are cases in point). PACs have probably been overrated as a lobbying resource for groups—contributions from any single group tend to be small and directed toward candidates who already agree with that group's position—but their importance will increase as they grow in number and gamble on replacing hostile incumbent representatives with challengers more sympathetic to their views.

While the percentage of voters in any district or state that is mobilized in this manner is very small, their political influence is magnified by their ability to deliver resources and to influence local public opinion. Congressmen have become more vulnerable or sensitive to these politically active constituents partly because of changes within Congress, particularly those which have increased the visibility of decisions. Open hearings and markups in committees and recorded teller votes on the floor have left Congress more permeable to these outside interests.

I hasten to add that members of Congress are far from waifs amid these forces. They still define themselves politically as they choose and ultimately determine who they will listen to; but they are now forced to answer to more groups on more issues, even if the answer is no.

### Implications for presidential leadership

As I suggested at the outset, there is a danger in reading too much into the consequences of recent changes in Congress for the relationship between the two branches. Conflict is a natural state of affairs; the periods of close cooperation have been rare. The problems now faced by presidents vis-à-vis the Congress are of a somewhat different order, but they are not new. John Kennedy was frustrated that the conservative coalition prevented a working Democratic majority on many issues and that a handful of powerful committee chairmen could block his legislative initiatives. Jimmy Carter confronts a Congress that is more difficult to manage—it's decentralized, individualized, open, frenetic, fluid and unpredictable—but one that gives him a chance to succeed where Kennedy would not have even tried.

Presidents now must deal with many more actors on Capitol Hill; they typically confront individuals and specialized groups rather than blocs and broad-gauged national organizations; presidents will also find it more difficult to make deals that will stick. This is the new reality. Presidents should acknowlege the inevitable messiness of the process and build that into their calculations and their rhetoric.

Since recent changes in the external environment have intensified the individualistic nature of members of Congress, presidents are best advised to treat members as independent political actors. Ignoring them or going over their heads to the Americcan public are actions doomed to failure. Any efforts to shape public opinion should be done in concert with members of Congress, not in conflict with them.

Changes in the structure of elections have greatly diminished the likelihood of government by authorization, in which the electoral ties between a president and his party's congressmen provide the additional votes and incentives to pass a program. Instead, we typically have government by representation, in which members motivated chiefly by their perceptions of the discrete interests they represent seek a compromise among these interests. Nonetheless, while presidential coattails have shortened or perhaps even vanished, and while the electoral bases of presidents and congressmen have become increasingly separated, presidents can still earn the respect of members of Congress. Public support, especially as registered in the polls, and demonstrated skill in dealing with the Washington community together increase the probability of success of presidential initiatives on Capitol Hill. The skill factor becomes increasingly important as Congress becomes more decentralized and individualized. And a president's approval ratings are watched closely by members attuned to the techniques of new-style campaigning.

In recent months it has become fashionable to bemoan the paralysis of American government, the inability of our political institutions to resolve controversial issues and to adopt policies that measure up to our most pressing national problems. For example, Lloyd Cutler, in a recent issue of *Foreign Affairs,* suggests various constitutional amendments that might help us "find a way of coming closer to the parliamentary concept of 'forming a Government,' under which the elected majority is able to carry out an overall program, and is held accountable for its success or failure."

While I agree that recent changes in Congress, both outside and within the institution, have blunted the instruments of collective accountability in our politics, I am not at all convinced that the symptoms justify radical surgery or that such surgery would improve the health of the patient. It is important to recognize that we have come through an historical period in which opportunities for individual participation were enhanced at the cost of diminishing the capacity of our political institutions. This is not unique to the U.S. Congress—similar trends can be observed in state legislatures, other national assemblies, the presidential nominating system, the family, and so on. While societal forces operating in the 1960s and 1970s worked against institutions, the 1980s may see a reversal of this trend.

In the meantime, presidents are well-advised, as Richard Fenno has observed, to seek out the institutionally-oriented members of Congress and to strengthen their hand in the legislative process. This reaching out to Congress must go well beyond the formal leaders, who are in no position to speak for their rank-and-file members. Presidents must harness the political energies and ambitions of a large and diverse set of congressmen who have a genuine interest in legislative outcomes. They must be knowledgeable about who to work with on Capitol Hill and skillful in developing productive relationships with them.

Many observers believe that the best hope for presidential-congressional cooperation lies with a revitalized political party system. They may be correct, but we are unlikely to see this formulation put to an empirical test. While in the last several years there have been impressive efforts—especially among the Republicans—to strengthen parties from the top, other forces, including television and the emergence of issues outside the New Deal public philosophy, are moving inexorably to weaken them. Even within this context, certain things could help to heighten concern for collective goals. A Republican takeover of the Senate and/or House would certainly sensitize members of the importance of the performance of their party, and not just their own electoral fate. But even here increased competition based not on the reputation of the parties but on more aggressive and attractive challengers will not necessarily alter the individualistic tone of the Congress. Much depends upon the success of the national parties' efforts to refocus public attention on the image and record of the parties.

Perhaps more promising is the possibility that a new set of political ideas will emerge in the next decade to give shape and substance to partisan competition. This revitalization would affect the context within which individuals are recruited to Congress and the climate in which they seek reelection. Such a change in the political atmosphere could improve conditions for governing in spite of the fragmented character of our political institutions. Yet, unlike a parliamentary system, our government can be severely weakened by unrestricted partisanship. The call for strong parties should not be too shrill—we need more partisan structure without a rigid and uncompromising partisanship.

# SOMETHING OLD, SOMETHING NEW:
## Lessons for a President about Congress in the Eighties

Norman J. Ornstein
*Professor of Political Science*
*Catholic University of America*

## I

Imagine that Sam Rayburn suddenly materializes on Capitol Hill, in January of 1980, nineteen years since he last set foot there. He would clearly be shocked, dismayed and stunned by much that he would see, and yet he would nod in instant recognition at many other things still going on much as they did two decades earlier. Looking more closely at the new Congress through Rayburn's eyes, the peculiar mix of continuity and change which have occurred during the past two decades, will enable us to sort out what has changed and what has not; to look at the kinds of problems this admixture of traditional and new elements poses for the White House; and to suggest ways in which future presidents might cope with them—indeed might even capitalize upon them.

## II

What would really surprise Rayburn in 1980? We can begin to answer the question by giving a capsulized description of what Mr. Sam was used to.

In the nineteen-fifties, Congress was a relatively slow-paced institution, dominated by its Committees and the senior leaders. It was insular also, in several respects. The inner workings of Congress and the decision process were not widely reported in the mass media or followed by many outside of Washington. Even in Washington, much that went on in the Capitol was unknown to outsiders who were shut out by closed door meetings and unrecorded votes. Prominence and power on the Hill were associated with long service. One travelled slowly up a ladder, angling for perquisites and rewards—foreign trips, coveted committee assignments, professional staff assistance, seats on conference committees—doled out by party leaders and committee chairmen, while awaiting one's turn to wield a gavel. Members not yet "arrived" were well advised to heed the informal "do's" and "don'ts": "keep quiet until you've been around long enough to know what you're talking about;" "be a workhorse, not a showhorse;" "to get along, go along;" "follow the lead of the experts on committees;" "maintain courtesy and mutual respect in debate."

Congressional behavior in the nineteen-fifties was quite predictable, at least to the cognocenti (including, of course, the Speaker). Bills from certain committees were certain to pass intact, bills from certain others to elicit intense controversy on the floor and amendment. Votes of most members were known long before the roll was actually called. Neither party nor ideology was a complete explanation, but together they told the close observer much about voting patterns. Most important, party leaders and committee chairmen were better able to control the events leading to legislative actions. When bills reached the floor, outcomes usually were already known to the schedulers. These outcomes tended to have been shaped behind closed doors, in committees, through coalitions led by committee chairmen (sometimes negotiated with party leaders) who used their own prestige, their control over committee resources and staff, and their power to enforce institutional norms for forging agreements either to kill a bill or to report it out behind a united committee front.

In a nutshell, Congress was a *closed* system characterized by clearly defined hierarchies with personal rewards and punishments and career incentives largely controllable from within the institution. Even members' standing with their electorates appears to have been significantly influenced by how well the members got ahead or got along inside Congress.

Compare such a Congress with today's. Congress in 1980, after a decade of internal reforms, explosive staff growth, intensive mass media attention, changes in the presidency and in interest groups, and with a majority of members elected during or after the Vietnam and Watergate years, is a fast-paced institution having hundreds of centers of activity and initiative—committees, sub-committees, individual members, staff. While stories on the institutional inner workings of Congress generally remain "EGO's" (eyes glaze over) to news editors, these myriad centers of activity on Capitol Hill are nevertheless sources of news for myriads of TV, radio, newspaper, newsletter and magazine reporters, who crowd hearing rooms and mark-up sessions and examine videotapes of the floor proceedings for excerpts for the nightly news. High-circulation magazines like *People* are as likely to feature attention-getting junior congressmen as Hollywood starlets. These members in turn are more likely to use their newly acquired celebrity status as a springboard to careers beyond Congress, in or out of politics. Some may be simply content to become desirable commodities on the Washington dinner party circuit. Others look on their congressional service as invaluable experience for their next jobs as Washington lawyers or lobbyists.

In the Congress of 1980, everybody takes foreign trips whenever they want, and nobody is denied a choice committee assignment. Indeed, some of the members most scornful of and disliked by the leadership are given seats as juniors on the prestigious Ways and Means or Foreign Relations committees. Chairmanships of subcommittees come early and often to majority members, and once-coveted committee chairmanships may have become to legislators what gas-guzzling Lincoln Continentals have become to consumers—not without their luxurious touches but hardly worth the expense to get them. All members, junior and senior, are furnished with staff for full-time work on administrative, legislative and constituency tasks, not to mention national and local press relations.

The traditional "do's" and "don'ts" heeded in the Rayburn era have disappeared. Members talk when they want and say what they want without fear of sanction or ostracism. The well-timed and well-received press release gets a member as much political credit as a diligent effort to mark up a bill. Criticizing Congress as an institution, its leaders or its members, or spurning the request of a party chieftain or committee chairman is acceptable, even approved behavior. Specialized expertise is ignored, doubted or vilified. Seniority is not esteemed by the majority of members who have served six years or less. Committee hegemony does not exist; amendments from outsiders are permitted, if not encouraged, and are certainly not rejected *a priori* as of yore.

Congress has become unpredictable to outsiders *and* insiders. No bill is safe from mutilation by amendment on the floor; the sources of the amendments are widespread and they often catch the bill's proponents by surprise. No votes are sure things; party whip counts are as stable as the price of gold. Ideology and party affiliation, taken separately or in combination, can serve to predict few outcomes. Decisions made in committees, whether unanimous or delicately balanced compromises, have no cachet any more on the floor. Moreover, bills cannot be killed quietly in committee, avoiding in advance a public embarrassment in the chamber. The committee meetings are open with cameras at the ready to maximize the attention given to committee defeat of a hospital cost containment bill, for example, or to committee censure of SALT.

This Congress, in short, is an *open* system. Power and activity are diffused, decentralized, shifting. There are as many rewards and incentives for members outside the institution as in; and within the legislature, rewards tend to be automatic, not doled out at the whim of a leader but obtained regardless of behavior, while no sanctions or punishments exist for bad deeds or violations of norms short of a felony. Members' electoral bases are enhanced by the universally distributed, generous allocation of resources in Congress. In fact, a member's credibility is usually bolstered by actions that flout the authority of congressional or presidential leadership or criticize Congress as a whole.

Decentralization and egalitarianism within Congress; vastly expanded congressional staff and information resources, now available to each individual member; the reduced importance of party affiliation, discretionary patronage, and deference to leaders as aids to congressional coalition-building: all these changes—probably irreversible in the near term—pose formidable obstacles for anyone who would try to lead Congress in the nineteen-eighties.

But it is important to recognize that Congress in the Rayburn era presented formidable obstacles to leadership also. The Speaker then was hardly all-powerful. Indeed, Speaker Rayburn had fewer tools of influence at his disposal than Speaker O'Neill has today, who unlike Rayburn enjoys power over committee assignments and control over the referral of bills. And Rayburn had to bow more often than not to the demands of recalcitrant committee chairmen, notably "Judge" Smith of the Rules Committee who buried bill after favored bill behind closed committee doors. (The big difference is that Rayburn's defeats were quiet ones or were stage-managed in a way that made them look like triumphs). Were he alive today, Rayburn might not consider it such a terrible trade-off to be rid of the Rules obstacle once and for all in exchange for greater difficulties in forging a majority on the floor.

It is important also to recognize that the recent changes in Congress, for all their antileadership tendencies, need not be fatal to the possibility of leadership in the nineteen-eighties. On the contrary, these changes may bring with them opportunites for leadership that were not present in the closed-system, seniority-dominated institution that was Congress in the nineteen-fifties.

What are those opportunities, and what does a President need to have and to do in order to exploit them in fulfilling his responsibilities for governance in the nineteen-eighties?

## III

First, the White House needs to recognize that most members of Congress will tend to respond to personal consideration and favors with consideration on their own part. Even if the "new breed" of legislator is predisposed to distrust leadership, has little or no intrinsic party loyalty, and cannot be regularly swayed by old-style carrots or pressured by old-style sticks, he or she is still a politician and a human being. Few are so vindictive as to stab a President deliberately in the back unless there is good political reason or unless they have been given cause for revenge. And most members—their professed cynicism notwithstanding—are still awed by the presidency and the White House. At the annual White House Christmas Ball for Congress in 1979 three hundred legislators stood in line, mashed together uncomfortably for twenty minutes or more waiting to shake hands with President Carter. The receiving line was not mandatory for them. They simply wanted to see and touch the leader.

A President and a White House staff who understand these realities can gain large leadership advantages through small actions to boost individual egos and enhance the political credit of individual members with their colleagues, the press, and their constituents. This does not require dazzling "charisma" on the President's part, nor does it require hard-boiled Johnsonian arm-twisting. It does require a well-organized, broad-based, smoothly administered program of activities responsive to the wide range of personalities and political needs of individual legislators: from special White House tours for favored constituents to the artful distribution of invitations to state dinners; from early notification to members of federal grant and contract awards in their districts to prompt responses to congressional letters and telephone calls. It requires a congressional liaison staff who make it their business to know which members need particular kinds of "ego massaging" and which ones don't, and to know which legislators are amenable to what kinds of carrots and sticks and when.

This is more difficult to do nowadays than it once was. In a de-centralized, egalitarian Congress made up of many individual political entrepreneurs, *all* members and many of the congressional staff people have to be "stroked" and responded to, not just a handful of elected party leaders or committee oligarchs. And even such a program, however smoothly administered, will by no means assure the White House of affirmative responses to its legislative initiatives. Nothing within the power of the White House could likely have prevented Congressmen Martin Russo (D-Ill.), for example, from undercutting President Carter in 1978 and killing the hospital cost containment bill.

But projecting a White House that is seriously trying to create an atmosphere of personal goodwill can give a President that small margin of special consideration—a "gimme" vote here and there, a bit of advance warning when a bill is in trouble or a needed vote is wavering, and some benefit of the doubt—that helps him maximize his own control over the staging and timing of legislative events, helps turn narrow defeats into narrow victories, or changes the tone on Capitol Hill from contempt to sympathy for the President when one of his policy initiatives fails.

Rubbing congresspeople the right way can also go far in dulling the edge of criticisms voiced to colleagues and to the media when they comment on presidential performance. The press reports that have plagued President Carter—many of them doubtless originating in Capitol cloakrooms—about congressional telephone calls unreturned and letters unanswered, about gaffes in extending invitations to White House functions, about anti-Carter Republican legislators announcing federal grants and getting the political credit before their Democratic counterparts had even heard of the awards, and about numerous other unintended but embarrassing slights to individual members, suffice to show how a reputation for inattentiveness or insensitivity in such matters gets propogated in today's open Congress, and greatly diminishes the personal respect, the political credit, and the public prestige that a president needs to command. Even though efforts have been made in the last two years to remedy these defects in White House congressional liaison, the negative perception of Mr. Carter as a leader of Congress that formed early in his presidency has lingered on to afflict his public relations and his relations with the Capitol ever since.

Second, the weakened power of the congressional leadership puts a premium on the President's skill in orchestrating the legislative process, focussing public and elite attention on major presidential bills, and timing critical legislative action on those bills when the climate is most favorable to passage. Lyndon Johnson and Sam Rayburn when they were serving in Congress were masters at delaying key votes until the right psychological and political moment had arrived. In the White House in 1964–65, President Johnson was astute in taking advantage of the momentum afforded by the tragedy of President Kennedy's assassination and by his own landslide victory to steamroll Great Society legislation through Congress. President Nixon timed his China trip and his announcement of a radical new policy departure with the People's Republic superbly to disarm his political adversaries and to capture world attention.

Obviously in the "new" Congress such feats of tactics and strategy are much more difficult to bring off than they once were. But the above examples show what can be gained by a president with a keen sense of timing and an appreciation of the need to invest considerable effort in legislative stage management. And President Carter's experience suggests the price that will be paid nowadays for White House inattentiveness to such matters. Consider, for example, how the first comprehensive energy bill was handled. In November of 1977 the President's bill was stalemated in Congress over the issue of natural gas pricing. Confronting this impasse, President Carter dramatically cancelled his four-continent world trip and announced that he would stay in Washington to get this "must" legislation passed. But he took this step, focussing public and world attention on the imperative need for action and putting his own reputation on the line, without having any plan to break the legislative deadlock. Not only that, but much evidence suggests that he let November go by without ever having a face-to-face session with the nine obstructing Senators. The result was to highlight his *inability* to get important legislation through Congress, to diminish enormously both his professional reputation in Washington and his public prestige, and to lose any credit for the success of the legislation six and a half months later when it was finally passed.

Much the same pattern was repeated in July of 1979 when the President abruptly cancelled his scheduled television talk on energy and "went to the mountain." When, following the intensive consultations at Camp David, he announced a major prime-time address, public interest and attention was very high. While the long-range energy program announce in that address was not greeted with wild enthusiasm, approval was the dominant public reaction. But instead of following through with actions to sustain that momentum on energy, the President announced two days later the firing of several cabinet members. Attention was diverted by this sensational news; energy policy disappeared from the headlines, forgotten; and once again his professional reputation suffered despite the ultimate success of an intensive, well-administered campaign to mobilize outside support for his energy bill coordinated by the White House public liaison staff.

Related to the heightened importance of legislative stage managing by the White House is the fact that Congress, partly because of internal fragmentation and egalitarianism, is finding it ever more difficult to manage its own workload or to bring coherence to its agenda. There may be little that the White House can do to remedy this problem in the nineteen-eighties. But there is much it can do to avoid exacerbating the problem of congressional overload and to minimize the possibility that important administration bills will get relegated to the end-of-session frenzy, or get lost in the shuffle altogether, or end up in competition with each other for congressional attention. In 1977 President Carter inundated Congress with more than a dozen pieces of major legislation, presented to the Hill in rapid succession. Many of these bills were technically complex or politically problematic or both; many of them descended almost all at once on the Ways and Means Committee; and there was apparently little effort by the White House to give any advance warning, to sort out the priorities among the bills, or to do the necessary political preparation. Presidents in the nineteen-eighties would be well advised to follow President Carter's later practice in controlling the number and sequence of presidential "must" bills—"prioritizing," as the practice has been called. They would be well advised also not to announce their legislative agenda until there has been an assessment, in consultation with the congressional leadership, of the degree of congressional attention each proposed bill is likely to command, both in the committees and on the floor, and the likelihood of passage.

It follows, as a third element of effective presidential-congressional relations, that the President will need a much strengthened congressional liaison staff and greater coordination within the White House staff in order to maintain leadership over the internally fragmented, activist, and lavishly staffed legislative branch in the nineteen-eighties.

As to strengthening of staff, the single greatest need will be to recruit individuals to the liaison staff, and preferably to other senior staff posts as well, who are experienced in the "legislative way of life" in Washington. Most Presidents have appointed at least one or two members of Congress to their cabinets. (President Carter began, for example, with Representative Bergland of Minnesota as Secretary of Agriculture and Representative Brock Adams of Washington as Secretary of Transportation). But because department heads tend to have vested policy and departmental interests of their own to protect, their congressional experience will not suffice to serve the President's needs in dealing with Capitol Hill. It is entirely in the interests of a President to recruit current and former members of Congress, as well as experienced and respected congressional staffers, to serve in senior White House staff positions, including the chief of the congressional liaison staff. The presence of such persons on the staff could serve to educate a President who might lack Washington experience about the congressional facts of life, and to build the congressional perspective into White House decision-making in advance of formal requests to Congress, as well as providing a core of expert tacticians who are essential for lobbying the President's bills through the political maze on Capitol Hill.

As to coordination within the White House, Presidents in the nineteen-eighties will need to recognize that congressional liaison has ceased to be—if it ever properly was—a discrete, separable staff function to be performed by a handful of congressional specialists. As has been recently recognized in President Carter's White House with the redirection and expansion of the public liaison staff under Anne Wexler, the nature of the "new" Congress requires much more outside lobbying than was needed in Rayburn's day, and much more coordination between the congressional liaison staff and the staff charged with mobilization of outside support, presidential bill by presidential bill. As the White House has also come lately to recognize, the changes in Congress require, in addition, more coordination between the policy staffs in the White House and the congressional liaison staff. The reason in part is that, with the vast expansion of congressional staff and information resources, Presidents can no longer rely as heavily as they have in the past on the marshalling of facts, figures, and policy experts to sway votes. In an era when hundreds of subcommitees and individual legislators have no great difficult marshalling their own, the White House can no longer expect to overpower Congress in this fashion. Indeed, reliance on such strategies may backfire when, as now occurs frequently, counter-facts, counter-figures, and counter-experts are mobilized on the Hill to challenge, openly and in front of television cameras, the President's technical competence and the credibility of his arguments.

Finally, fragmentation on Capitol Hill increases the need for hierarchy—or at least for leadership—inside the White House. Presidents who adhere to the Rooseveltian, "spokes of the wheel" staff system will do so at their peril in dealing with Congress in the nineteen-eighties: for a decentralized or disorganized Executive Office cannot deal effectively with a decentralized or disorganized Congress at the other end of Pennsylvania Avenue. This new fact of life, too, has lately come to be recognized by the White House with the establishment of a chief of staff position. Such a position offers the best insurance that the necessary coordination will be achieved among the special staffs or staff individuals whose activities have congressional consequence—from the handling of appointments to the construction of White House invitation lists, from the arrangement of grants and grant announcements to the scheduling of presidential appearances and the writing of speeches and press releases, from policy development to policy salesmanship.

One further thought: Presidents might be well advised to consider trying to move the government to a two-year budget cycle. Many of today's presidential-congressional clashes come over the budget—over the economic assumptions underlying the budget recommendations as well as over specific priorities and items in the budget. Given the prospect of continuing high political salience of economic and budgetary issues, these clashes are not likely to lessen in the foreseeable future, and may indeed intensify and spill over into other substantive areas. Moreover, given the deadlines established by the 1974 Budget Act, budget and appropriations matters are consuming ever-larger quantities of congressional time. A two-year budget cycle might lessen the current focus on budget-related conflicts, allow more space and time on the congressional agenda for other matters, and give the President more opportunities for establishing that reputation for winning on the Hill that is vitally important to the maintenance of his leadership. A President's losses do not look as bad if they occur half as often.

– – – – –

Future Presidents will find Congress frustrating, confusing, capricious and challenging. Past Presidents found Congress frustrating, confusing, capricious and challenging. Enough has changed in the past decade or so to make the confusion different and the challenge more formidable, perhaps, but the changes also offer a President new opportunites and openings for influence in Congress. A combination of old political skills applied in new ways can make a future President at least as pleased with his relations with Congress as were past "giants" as FDR and LBJ.

# THE STAFF OF INDEPENDENCE:
## Why Congress Employs More But Legislates Less

Allen Schick
School of Public Affairs
The University of Maryland

When Edmund Muskie moved from the Senate to the State Department, he suffered a great decline in the number of persons directly serving him. As a Senator, Muskie probably had more people working for him than did Zbigniew Brzezinski, the President's national security adviser, whom Secretary of State Muskie would later regard as a rival with an overreaching staff. By virtue of his seniority and committee posts, Muskie had more staff under his command than did many of his Senate colleagues, but like all Members of Congress he drew staff from a variety of sources. Some were assigned to his office by a population-based formula; some were employed by the Environmental Pollution subcommittee which he chaired; and some served the Foreign Relations Committee. The largest number worked for the Senate Budget Committee.

Although the numbers vary from Member to Member, personal and committee staff comprise the bulk of congressional employees. Table 1 shows that more than 17,000 persons work directly for Members and committees, thousands more are employed by congressional support agencies, and another 3,500 serve in "housekeeping" positions. Overall, Congress employs more persons to care for Capitol Hill than the State Department does for the conduct of diplomatic relations around the world.

Congress does not live by staff alone, but it would be a radically different institution if it were not overrun by legions of case workers, personal aides, legislative assistants, secretaries, Capitol police, and all the rest. Congressional staff spread to every corner of the legislative process. Except for fleeting exchanges on the floor, usually during roll calls, Members rarely get together without staff to discuss legislative business. It would be hard to imagine a contemporary Congress in action unaided (or unfettered) by staff.

This essay explores the causes and effects of what Michael Malbin has termed "unelected representatives." While there are many reasons for the growth of congressional staff, I shall concentrate on two: relations between Congress and the President and the distribution of power within Congress. These also will be the principal factors in considering the effects of staff growth on the conduct of government.

### Congressional Staff as a Response to Executive Power

Big legislative staffs are a distinctively American phenomenon. In the early 1970s, the British House of Commons and the German Bundestag averaged one staff aide for each legislator. The 635 Members of Commons shared a 55-person research staff, while committees had 48 employees. The 518-member Bundestag had larger had larger committee and research staffs (257 and 156 respectively) but these were much smaller than the comparable congressional staffs.[1]

Clearly, staff size is less a function of multiple membership than of the political conditions under which a national legislature operates. Although there are many relevant differences between presidential government in the United States and parliamentary democracy elsewhere, the most salient one for this analysis is the division of national power between the executive and legislative branches. Congress would not have employed hordes of assistants if its political fate had been joined with the executive's by Cabinet government, strong party discipline, and shared accountability to the electorate. Separation of powers has impelled Congress to build its own staff resources in order to maintain independence from the executive branch. Gladys Kammerer expressed the perennial justification for more staff when she urged staff expansion in order for Congress to "function as a coequal partner with the executive."[2] In its own eyes, Congress adds staff in re-

---

[1] Gerhard Loewenberg and Samuel C. Patterson, *Comparing Legislatures* (Boston: Little, Brown & Co., 1979), p. 161.

[2] Gladys Kammerer, "The Record of Congress in Committee Staffing," *American Political Science Review* (Dec., 1951), p. 1126.

sponse to prior developments in the executive branch.

The chief development has been the growth of government itself. Congress would not have acquired a 20th-century staff if the national government had continued to operate within a 19th-century scope. Conversely, if Congress had restricted itself to a 19th-century staff, it could not have claimed political parity with a 20th-century executive. Government expansion has meant more executive actions to monitor and more policies to formulate or review.

Governmental growth also has meant more executive staff for Congress to deal with. Herbert Kaufman's study on organizational change in 10 executive departments and the Executive Office of the President found that 42 percent of the organizations established between 1923 and 1973 were staff units. Despite the vast enlargement of the federal government's operations, 38 percent of the organizations were staff units in 1973, up from a level of 28 percent 50 years earlier.[3] Moreover, an increasing proportion of line agency employees occupy staff positions. Over the years, major federal agencies have added their own information specialists, lawyers, finance officers, policy analysts, and other staff personnel.

When Members of Congress think about staff, they often see themselves disadvantaged vis-à-vis the executive branch. Most federal department heads have their own administrative and executive assistants, public affairs experts, congressional liaison, and other aides. A typical Cabinet member has someone to handle appointments, someone else to screen incoming and outgoing mail, a speechwriter, and at least one person to deal with Congress. The immediate staff of a department head might add up to fewer persons than are on a congressman's payroll, but Members of Congress believe that they have fewer staff resources at their command. These perceptions are reinforced by instances in which Members have to deal with agency staff rather than with the department secretary. Members sometimes have their access blocked by an aide who controls the secretary's time. They sometimes are compelled to negotiate with anonymous aides who purport to represent the department head. These "indignities" might be infrequent occurrences, but Members sense a mismatch in status between the legislative and executive branches. The proper

---

[3] Herbert Kaufman, *Are Government Organizations Immortal?* (Washington: The Brookings Institution, 1976), p. 38.

solution from a congressional vantage point is to add legislative staff.

Daniel Moynihan has labelled the process by which Congress adapts to executive behavior as the "Iron Law of Emulation":

> Whenever any branch of the government acquires a new technique which enhances its power in relation to the other branches, that technique will soon be adopted by those other branches as well.[4]

Moynihan formulated his law of emulation to explain why, in his view, an imperial presidency has led to an imperial Congress. He thus characterizes the formation of the Congressional Budget Office during the 1970s as a response to the establishment of the President's Bureau of the Budget more than 50 years earlier. The old Bureau, he argues, "gave the President an enormous advantage over the Congress." But with its own budget office, Congress could achieve "a rough equivalence of competence with respect to the techniques of fiscal management and disputation."[5]

Emulation is a form of political competition. Just as firms compete by offering similar products or services (note the similar models offered by Detroit automakers, the clustering of transcontinental flights at the same time, and imitation in television programs) so, too, politicians protect their interests by adopting the tactics used by their rivals. If Congress is more imitative than the executive branch, it is because Congress is less powerful. The branch that commands the initiative leads; others follow.

Once a staff resource is successfully used in the executive branch, Congress can be expected to replicate it. Thus, during the past decade, Congress has been busy adding its own computer systems, programmers, and information specialists. Between 1970 and 1979, the House Administration Committee's staff grew from 25 to 266, largely because of the expansion of its House Information Systems. Following a similar development in the executive branch, Congress has equipped its committees and staff agencies with policy analysts and program evaluators.

Emulating the executive branch requires a huge legislative staff, if only because Congress is composed of hundreds of Members and committees. Most Members want their own appointments

---

[4] Daniel P. Moynihan, "An Imperial Presidency Leads to an Imperial Congress Leads to an Imperial Judiciary: The Iron Law of Emulation," printed in 124 *Congressional Record* (daily ed. August 1, 1978) S. 12291-5.

[5] *Ibid.*

secretary and a press secretary, a few aides to keep in touch with the grass roots and a few for casework, at least one or two for legislative business, and someone to take care of committee responsibilities. These "basic" needs require congressional staff numbering in the thousands. Yet many Members feel inadequately staffed and have to make difficult trade-offs among competing demands. If they shift staff to district offices, they might be short-handed in Washington; if they concentrate on services to con-stituents, they might have to curtail their legislative activity. One reason why congressional staffs grow is that Members seek to function in multiple roles without trading away one resource for another.

As the most visible and powerful symbol of executive leadership, the President is an influential object of emulation. Members of Congress see the President attended by an entourage of assistants who ease his path, execute his will, and deal with those inside and outside government who have White House business. The President has loyal aides watching out for his interests; he never travels alone; he never wants for someone to carry out his orders. Emulative Members of Congress also need their own entourages. Though much smaller, congressional entourages have functions similar to those performed by the President's.

In order to match the executive Branch in status, Congress needs a palace guard. The 1100-member Capitol police force, one of the largest in the United States, protects both congressional property and status. Police are everywhere on Capitol Hill, usher-ing people in and keeping people out, opening up a convenient path to the elevator and the Capitol subway, making sure that Members don't have to wait for others, and according them the recognition due national leaders.

Although it is widespread, emulation is not an assured or auto-matic congressional response. The speed and extent to which Congress matches executive actions depend on the political re-lationship between the two branches, especially on Congress' yearning for independence. Although the Constitution structured a government of separated powers, it also created, as Richard Neustadt and others have noted, a need for cooperation and shared powers. The constitutional license for legislative indepen-dence is hedged by the practical need to get along and by the political fact of the President's dominant position in the American scheme of things. As long as it is willing to be dependent on the executive, Congress might be satisfied with modest staffs of its own. As a dependent branch, Congress can legitimately rely on executive staff for legislative proposals, data and analyses, and services to constituents. But when Members strive for political independence, they want to perform these tasks themselves, In building its own informational and analytic resources, Congress has been swayed by the argument that it should not be dependent on executive data or executive interpretations. With staff of its own, Congress can make its own assumptions, develop its own alternatives, and draw its own conclusions.

The congressional striving for independence has varied over time and among participants in the legislative process. The 53-year lag from establishment of the Bureau of the Budget to formation of the Congressional Budget Office was due, in large measure, to the willingness of the Appropriations Committees—particularly House Appropriations—to depend on the President's budget aides. As one of the most executive-oriented committees in Congress, House Appropriations usually acted only pursuant to a presidential initiative such as submission of the annual budget. It measured each appropriations decision in terms of the President's recommendation. For each account, Appropriations reported the amount requested by the President, its recommendation, and the variance between the two figures. Although it regularly claimed great success in cutting the President's budget, the committee usually made comparatively modest changes.

The Appropriations Committees had no need for an independent budget staff in Congress. On request, they were able to get any information they wanted from executive agencies. Moreover, when they needed additional staff for investigations, these committees looked to executive agencies (such as the FBI) for temporary "details." Of course, other congressional committees were not similarly privileged, and their demands for a broader budgetary perspective and a more independent legislative stance led to the congressional budget process and the creation of a budget staff on Capitol Hill.[6]

The House and Senate Armed Services Committees provide a more enduring illustration of congressional acquiescence in a dependent relationship. Despite the critical importance of national security and the large share of the budget claimed by defense

---

[6] For a discussion of the development of the congressional budget process, see Allen Schick, *Congress and Money: Budgeting, Spending, and Taxing* (Washington: The Urban Institute: 1980).

programs, these committes have small staffs. As reported in Table 2, the House Armed Services Committee ranks 18th out of 22 House Committees in staff size; the Senate Armed Services has next to the smallest committee staff in the Senate. This writer recalls the time he questioned the staff director of one of the Armed Services Committees about the committee's supply of information and analyses. "We never have trouble getting what we want," the staff director replied, pointing to his copy of the Pentagon telephone directory.

Some committees assert their independence after an extended period of reliance on the executive branch. Such was the case with the House International Relations and the Senate Foreign Relations Committees. During the heyday of bipartisanship in foreign policy after World War II, these committees had small staffs, about the same size as those of the Armed Services Committees. Whatever the virtues of bipartisanship, this once-powerful political norm deterred Congress from taking an independent stance in foreign policy. After Vietnam, however, bipartisanship was eroded and Congress often challenged the President on foreign policy. The two foreign policy committees enlarged their staffs, and these are about twice the size of the Armed Services staffs.

There is a tide to congressional independence, but it does not flow in regular, predictable cycles. One obvious influence is the extent to which Congress and the White House are controlled by the same party. During almost half the years (16 of 34) since 1946, political control has been divided, providing Congress with a strong incentive for staff expansion. When party unity has been restored, growth usually has levelled off, but Congress has not rolled back staff increases.

A more important, though less tangible factor, is Congress' perception of its role. Congressional dependence is sometimes deemed a virtue, as it was during the early Johnson years when Great Society legislation was rushed into law. During the 1970s, Congress saw its proper role as a check on executive power, and its political resurgence was reflected in enormous staff growth. Member and committee staffs doubled in size during the decade, and staff increases also occurred in the congressional support agencies, two of which were formed during the 1970s.

The "billion-dollar" Congress label which was pinned on Congress late in the decade was not only a statement about the cost of the legislative branch but also a questioning of its role and independence. It suggested that the tide in legislative-executive relations had begun to turn, as it had during other periods in American history. In place of the earlier protests about the imperial presidency, concern was now voiced about an imperiled presidency and an imperial Congress. If this attitude takes root on Capitol Hill, it will certainly be reflected in the staffing of Congress.

### Congressional Staff as a Redistribution of Legislative Power

Congress is not a homogeneous institution with a single or consistent set of interests. Even in its relations with the executive branch, Congress speaks with multiple voices. Although Members and committees argue for more staff by claiming disadvantage vis-à-vis the executive branch, when Congress adds staff it tends to be more interested in the redistribution of legislative power than in the division of power between the two branches.

The growth of congressional staffs is very much part of the story of what happened to Congress during the 1970s. In the 1980s, Congress is a much more open but less disciplined institution than it was in the previous decade. Power is much more widely diffused, and junior Members participate more actively and successfully than they once did. Floor amendments are much more numerous, and there are many more roll calls in the House and Senate than once was the case. These changes in the legislative process have been facilitated by a wider distribution of staff resources. Power in Congress would not be widely shared if access to staff were concentrated in a few hands.

As a collegiate institution with a low tolerance for intramural conflict, Congress is inclined to give each interest what it wants most. If one component of the legislative branch wants more staff, the total supply of staff is increased, thus satisfying that interest without expressly disadvantaging others. Staff, in short, are added, not reallocated. Although the net effect might be redistributive, Congress behaves in a distributive style. Understandably, distributive staffing policies lead to continuing increases in overall staff size.

It wasn't very long ago that Congress embraced the notion that everybody gains from adequate legislative staff. The institution as a whole would benefit if Members and committees were better informed and prepared to discharge their legislative responsibility. This *pro bono* view of staff was accepted by the 1970 Legislative Reorganization Act which provided modest staff increases for committees (two additional aides each) but called for a tripling of the Congressional Research Service staff. "In the long run," the House Rules Committee declared, "it will be both less expensive and more productive to build up these supplementary research staffs than to disperse additional special staff among the committees."[7] As a pooled resource, CRS would be available to all committees and Members, thereby satisfying the analytical and informational needs of Congress.

But, as things turned out, a staff pool was not the only thing Congress needed. CRS added 500 positions during the 1970s, but committee and Member staffs still grew apace during the decade. The redistributive effects of staffing changes push Congress to augment staff in many quarters. One group succeeds in getting more resources, another counters with its own claims. In a political environment, satisfying one interest spurs others to take protective measures.

*Congressional Budgeting: A Profile in Staff Enlargement.* The Congressional Act of 1974 came only four years after the 1970 Reorganization Act, but Congress was no longer under the illusion that more staff was a blessing for all. By 1974, staff was openly seen as an instrument of legislative power. Accordingly, the Budget Act generated a great deal of internal conflict over the distribution and "ownership" of budget staff. The original design (proposed by the Joint Study Committee on Budget Control) recognized that Congress needed its own budget staff but sought to avert a redistribution of legislative staff by providing for a joint staff to serve the new House and Senate Budget Committees. Since these committees would have been dominated by the tax and appropriations committees (which would have named two thirds of the members and the chairman), the new staff would, it was hoped, be controlled by the exisiting powerholders. The proposed budget staff was modeled after the Joint Committee on Taxation which serves as the staff arm of the House Ways and Means and Senate Finance Committees. Congress, under the proposal, would not have its own budget office. Although no official projections were made of the joint staff's expected size, the feeling among those who drafted the original proposal was that it would be small, more like a committee staff than a distinct unit.

The proposal was attacked by congressmen who wanted wider

---

[7] H. Rept. No. 91-1215 (June 17, 1970), p. 19.

distribution of legislative power. The Democratic Study Group warned against establishing a "super" committee that would dictate budget policy to Congress. Members outside the appropriations-tax committee orbit sought assurance that they would have ready access to budget experts and data. Some senators pushed for a separate staff that would undertake independent studies and offer alternatives to the President's budget.

These differing points of view found a compromise in the Budget Act. Each Budget Committee was to have its own staff; in addition, the Congressional Budget Office would be a nonpartisan staff agency. But the new budget office would be governed by an explicit set of priorities written into law. First claim on its resources would go to the Budget Committees; the tax and appropriations committees would be next in line; after these priorities were satisfied, the budget office could assist other legislative committees. Finally, Members would be entitled only to available material, but they could not request new research.

The distributive push for additional staff continued after the Budget Act took effect. The House Appropriations Committee sought to protect its status by adding more than 30 employees between 1975 and 1979. Most authorizing committees hired their own budget experts because they did not want to be dependent on the Budget Committees for information or analyses. The Budget Committees rapidly built unexpectedly large staffs—more than 80 positions each—enabling them to keep watch over the activities of other committees. The Congressional Budget Office sought to ensure its independence from the demands of the budget process and congressional committees by planning for 259 positions, many more than the size foreseen when the Budget Act was being developed. CBO's plans were trimmed back by suspicious Appropriations Committees, but it still obtained more than 200 staff slots. The General Accounting Office, which for years had accorded low priority to budget analyses, entered into the competition by setting up its own program analysis staff. When the dust had settled, the budget process had added approximately 500 persons to Congress' staff rolls.

*Members versus chairmen.* Legislators covet staff because it is the currency with which they secure independence. In the 1970s, Members sought independence from committee chairmen, committee jurisdictions, and political parties. Each of these strivings for independence led to staff expansion.

At one time—until the 1960s for most committees—committee staff worked for the chairman. The chairman hired and fired, told the staff what to do, and defined their legislative aspirations. Staff did not provide substantial assistance to rank-and-file Members without clearing it with the chairman. Under these circumstances, chairmen saw little gain in enlarging their staffs. With only a handful of committee employees, there was little risk that staff would act independently. Moreover, small staffs were deemed to be a legislative virtue, for elected representatives rather than appointed employees would be directly involved in the legislative process. This attitude was more strongly held in the House than in the Senate and was reflected in different staff patterns in the two chambers. In 1947, House committees averaged only 8 employees each; Senate committees averaged twice that number.

With small staffs, chairmen dominated the legislative process. Members often came to markup without precise information on the matters to be decided. Many committees strictly limited attendance by staff; some, such as Ways and Means, barred aides of Member staffs. In markup, the chairman would circulate draft legislation and move the committee to approve his recommendation with few changes. Rank-and-file had limited input, and there was little doubt as to who was in charge.

The pattern described here did not prevail with equal force in all committees, but it was sufficiently pervasive to stand as a generalization concerning the distribution of power and staff in Congress. Clearly, however, it does not fit the current practices of most congressional committees. With only few exceptions, the era of dominant chairmen is over. Though no single factor accounts for their decline, the expansion of congressional staffs has been a key factor. Staff growth made it more difficult for the chairman to control what employees did and made it easier for Members to get assistance. The proliferation of subcommittees was followed by the proliferation of subcommittee staffs. In many instances, subcommittees surpassed their parent committee in staff size. More importantly, the subcommittee chief—not the full committee chairman—controlled the subcommittee staff. Members demanded—and often got—their own subcommittees in order to get their own staffs. The House had 8 subcommittees in 1955; in 1975 it had 155. The Senate grew from 94 to 157 subcommittees during the same period. Although subcommittee expansion gave senior Members their own staffs, it did not always mean more staff for junior congressmen. In 1975, however, the Senate adopted S. Res. 60, entitling all senators to staff assistance for each committee assignment. The House does not have a comparable entitlement, but many House committees now have staff aides for their members. Further erosion of the chairman's dominance came with the opening of committee meetings to the public. Chairman could no longer bar personal aides once the public was permitted to attend.

It is now common for committee rooms to be jammed with staff during markup. With their own aides at hand to help with legislation and other business, Members no longer have to rubber stamp the chairman's recommendations. Rank-and-file can exercise their own judgment and offer amendments to draft legislation. Some committees have adjusted to this new reality by staging "staff markups" before the committee considers legislation. These informal sessions are not governed by sunshine rules, nor are votes normally taken in them. The group operates by consensus, with Democrats and Republicans both having a say. The purpose of these staff meetings is to touch all bases and iron out problems or disagreements before the committee meets in the open. Staffs speak for Members by suggesting changes in proposed legislation or by offering amendments on matters of interest to their principals. In some committees, the chairman will not schedule a markup until the legislation has been cleared at the staff level. Rather than risk opposition or unexpected amendments, the chairman is willing to delay markup until staff have ironed out their problems. And even if full agreement cannot be achieved before markup, the staff sessions serve to narrow the range of conflicts and identify those items that the Members will have to vote on in markup.

By organizing committee work in this fashion, a chairman can retain a semblance of control in markup. But the price for procedural control can be the loss of substantive control over the legislation. The chairman doesn't "write" the bill anymore. On major legislation, he must accept amendments offered by other committee members in order to get their support. He will add "non-germane" matters to the bill when pressed by colleagues who have their own interests. He will agree to amendments which aren't properly integrated with the rest of the bill because he would rather have a jerry-built, poorly-drafted, redundant, and sometimes contradictory measure than renegotiate understandings with congressional peers.

These tendencies are more pronounced in the Senate than in the House, but the changes have been more significant in the latter. Senators have long been accustomed to delegating substantial responsibility to staff; many representatives still take pride in working directly on legislation and negotiating with colleagues. But the tide is running against their direct involvement in the drafting of legislation, and representatives increasingly rely on staff for basic legislative work. A comparison of committee staff size shows increased use of staff in the House. As recently as 1960, Senate committee staffs were larger than those of the House. Since then, however, House committee staffs have quadrupled in size, and almost twice as many people are now employed by House Committees than by the Senate's.

*Independence from committees.* The status of a chairman in committee affects the status of a committee in its parent chamber. When the chairman rules, the committee can come to the floor united in behalf of its recommendations, and it can move the legislation through the House or Senate with little difficulty. But when the committee is divided and the chairman cannot speak for it on matters in contention, the committee can expect to have difficulty selling its product to the large number of congressmen who don't sit on it. The weakening of leadership in committee has weakened the status of committees as congressional specialists in their respective jurisdictions.

In the past, committee assignments shaped the legislative interests of most Members. Senators and representatives attained power on the floor by being recognized as specialists in their particular fields of legislation. Specialization had a number of virtues: it distributed legislative power widely, at least among senior Members, and simplified the voting responsibilities of Members. Members could not become experts on every issue facing them, nor could they be equally informed on every matter presented for their vote. But by deferring to legislative specialists, usually colleagues from the committee of jurisdiction, Members could act in a responsible manner. Specialization also simplified the decision-making processes of the House and Senate. With

Members active only within their specializations, there was little danger that measures would be attacked on the floor by "outsiders" who were not party to the deliberations in committee.

By simplifying the legislative agendas of Members and chambers, specialization also limited the demand for congressional staff. Members did not need aides to help them on every matter up for decision in committee or on the floor. Not only could Members vote by cue, but there were fewer issues to vote on since non-specialists were wary about openly challenging the congressional experts. More than 1,000 public laws were enacted by the 84th Congress, but during that two-year period (1955–56) there were only 147 record votes in the House and 224 in the Senate.

Specialization still is an important element in the legislative process—a collegial body would be hard-pressed to complete its business if all Members were deemed to be equally authoritative on every issue—but it certainly is not as pervasive as it once was. Specialization thrives in a "nondecisional" environment (executive sessions, closed rules, nonrecord votes, etc.) but is difficult to maintain when any Member can force an issue. Specialization also depends on reasonably clear demarcations of legislative responsibilities. If Members are unsure or fighting among themselves as to who is responsible for legislation, it is difficult for cue-takers to know whom to follow. The proliferation of subcommittees has blurred jurisdictional boundaries, for by establishing new subunits Members can stake their legislative claim over matters that might be in another committee's bailiwick. The steep rise in multiple referrals, instances in which more than one committee has jurisdiction, suggests that specializations are not as clearly defined—or adhered to—as once was the case. In some extreme cases—energy policy is perhaps the most extreme—just about every standing committee claims some involvement. If everyone acts as a specialist, no one is.

The decline of specialization has gone hand in hand with the growth of legislative staffs. Members have to compensate for the lack of cues by voting on the basis of information; they need legislative aides to identify the issues and advise them on how to vote. Members also have to vote much more often. There were more than 2,500 record votes in the 94th Congress (1975–76), 7 times the number in the 84th Congress. With this enormous increase, Members can have more staff than before, yet feel more inadequately staffed. The rise in workload occasioned by weakened specialization spreads to many facets of the legislative process. There were twice as many committee and subcommittee meetings in the 94th Congress than there were in the 84th. The amount of time in session also increased, though not as steeply. But declining specialization means that fewer bills have safe passage through the House and Senate. The 94th Congress managed to approve barely half the number of measures enacted in the 84th.

Members are not simply passive victims of declining specialization who plead for more staff in order to cope with the difficult situation. They exploit the loss of specialization by becoming more active participants in legislative matters outside their committee assignments. Nowadays, little opprobrium attaches to Members who offer floor amendments to bills out of committees other than their own. Indeed, Members scan the calendars for "vehicles" onto which they can attach amendments. They demand more staff to get what might be termed legislative extraterritoriality, the capability to function successfully in areas outside their committee assignments.

*The political independence of Members.* Members not only have larger staffs, they deploy them differently. At one time, virtually all personal aides worked in Washington, but there was a marked shift of staff to district and state offices during the 1970s. In 1972, approximately 1,500 congressional employees were assigned to field offices; by 1979, the number had climbed to more than 3,300. Approximately 30 percent of Member staffs were stationed in the field in 1979 compared to 20 percent in 1972.

Field staff do casework, and they do political work. Serving as brokers and ombudsmen they handle complaints and inquiries from constituents. They distribute press releases and supply the media with a flow of news about the Member's activities in Washington. They work with local officials to get grants from federal agencies and with businesses to get contracts. In short, they do the kinds of things that party organizations used to do.

Many local offices serve as proto-campaign staffs, especially for House Members who have only two years between elections. Although many Members maintain a proper legal demarcation between congressional and campaign staff, the things that congressional employees do year round are quite similar to the tasks performed by campaign workers before elections. Working with their home-based staffs, Members often have mobile offices or storefronts which are easily accessible to constituents. These local offices are a political base for Members who in the jet age return home much more frequently than their counterparts did in past generations. With a local staff in place, Members can productively use recesses and weekends to meet constituents and prepare for the next election. In effect, Members can run a continuous campaign while still tending to their legislative responsibilties. It should be noted that despite the growth of district and state staffs, Members employ more aides in Washington than they did a decade ago.

If parties once were service organizations, Congress has now become a service institution. In an age of big government, this might be an appropriate adaptation for Congress, particularly since it abets the electoral aspirations of Members. With constituent services reaching out to their districts and states, Members can, in Richard Fenno's perceptive phrase, run for Congress by running against Congress. As much as they might hold Congress in low esteem, many voters nevertheless see their representative as a leader responsive to their needs.

There is one noticeable difference between a district office and party headquarters: there are few, if any, identifications of party in Member offices. But if party appears to mean so little back home, can it mean more for Members in Congress? When a Member has earned reelection by dint of his own efforts, it is difficult for the party to call him to account.

Local offices have not preempted party organizations; they have filled a political void. The decline of parties began long before the growth of field staffs. One can expect continued expansion of these staffs during the 1980s, but it is possible that rather than fostering more independence from parties, they might have the opposite effect. To the extent that permanent field staff strengthen their election prospects, Members of Congress might feel freer to vote the party line, except, of course, on matters of critical importance to their constituencies.

*The Problem with Independence*

Independence comes to Congress at a high price, not merely the financial costs of payrolls and office expenses but the political costs of hobbling the ability of Congress to work with the executive branch and the ability of Members to work with one another. In an age of interdependence, staff might increase the effectiveness of individual Members while damaging the effectiveness of government.

The President's legislative role has been vastly complicated by the growth of legislative staff. More Members are involved in the making of legislation, but fewer have control over the outcome. The President cannot consult with all who are interested in a measure, nor can he be sure that those with whom he has negotiated can deliver the votes. Goaded by their staff, Members conduct more hearings, demand more testimony from high executive officials, counter presidential proposals with their own alternatives, and challenge executive reports with their own figures and analyses.

In the best of times, the President bridges the constitutional chasm by building trust between the White House and the legislative branch. The key building blocks of political trust are interpersonal relations and adherence to commitments and understandings. The President cannot win congressional confidence by dealing with the legislature as a mass, but neither can he establish personal ties to each of the hundreds who participate in the legislative process. Presidents overcome this dilemma by dealing with congressional leaders who, in turn, convey a sense of trust to rank-and-file. But the growth of staff is part of the decline of leadership in Congress. Not only have committee chairmen been dethroned, but party leaders lack the leverage exercised by their predecessors. It is noteworthy that leadership staffs in Congress have not grown as much as those of Members and Committees.

If leaders cannot deliver, a President can try to forge understandings by consulting with a wider band of legislators. The trouble with this strategy, however, is that the more side deals that a President must make, the more misunderstanding he sows. Lacking permanent allies, the President will be forced to make do with a shifting coalition, depending on the issues and the times. This is not an easy prospect for a President who has a lot of other things on his mind, but the alternative used by some recent chief executives—trying to browbeat Congress into submission—does not work. A Congress of independents does not submit so easily to threats and bombast.

Nor can a Congress of independents work as an effective institution. There are more blockage points in committee and on the floor, more Members whose objections or doubts can lead to delay. With the leadership so uncertain as to what awaits legislation on the floor, it lowers its sights and tries to curb the appetite of Members for more business. The legislation which makes it to the floor is legislation which cannot be kept off the floor, principally appropriations, extension of expired authorizations, and other "must" legislation.

More staff and less specialization combine for more amendments but fewer laws. It is harder for the leadership to "scenario" floor debate, but more urgent to do so. Legislative input increases while legislative output declines. Congess works harder but produces less. Staff, which once seemed to be the solution, now are seen as part of the problem. With more eyes and ears to patrol committee agendas and floor calendars, Members can accomplish more for themselves though their institution's legislative capability might be impaired.

The old days are gone. Congress will not return to the closed system it once was. Even if Congress wanted to do so, the mobilization of outside interests and attention would deter it from closing off many avenues of opportunity and independence for its members. Yet Congress has to compose itself for the conduct of legislative business and for the sharing of governmental power and responsibility with the executive branch. While the evidence is uncertain, it appears that Congress is moving to leash its independence and that of its Members. There has been a pronounced dropoff in the growth rate of congressional staffs. House and Senate committees added 1,270 employees between 1971 and 1975; during the next four years, they added only 340. A similar trend appears in the staffing of Member offices and support agencies. If staff buy independence, a slowdown in its growth might signal a return to a more dependent Congress. If one looks back far enough in congressional history, one would be able to look far enough ahead to predict that the pendulum will shift again.

When? It's already started, but at the rate things are going, it might take quite a while until the tilting point is reached.

## TABLE 1

## CONGRESSIONAL STAFF, 1972 AND 1979

*Number of Employees*

| | 1972 | 1979 | %<br>Change |
|---|---|---|---|
| Member Staff | | | |
| House District Offices | 1,189 | 2,445 | 105.6 |
| Total House Member Staff | 5,280 | 7,067 | 33.8 |
| Senate State Offices | 303 | 879 | 190.0 |
| Total Senate Member Staff | 2,426 | 3,612 | 48.9 |
| Committee Staff | | | |
| House Committees | 817 | 1,959 | 139.8 |
| Senate Committees | 844 | 1,098 | 30.1 |
| Leadership Staff | | | |
| House | 80 | 113* | 41.3 |
| Senate | 52 | 80* | 53.8 |
| Offices of the House Staff | 1,478 | 1,462* | − 1.1 |
| Offices of the Senate Staff | 952 | 1,317* | 38.3 |
| Congressional Support Agencies | | | |
| General Accounting Office | 4,742 | 5,303 | 11.8 |
| Congressional Research Service | 479 | 847 | 76.8 |
| Congressional Budget Office | — | 207 | NA |
| Office of Technology Assessment | — | 145 | NA |

*Data for 1978

Sources: John F. Bibby, Thomas E. Mann & Norman J. Ornstein, *Vital Statistics on Congress 1980* (Washington: American Enterprise Institute) and Judy Schneider, "Congressional Staffing: 1947–1978" (Congressional Research Service, August 24, 1979).

## TABLE 2a

## STAFF SIZE OF HOUSE COMMITTEES SELECTED YEARS

| House Committees | 1947 | 1960 | 1970 | 1975 | 1979 |
|---|---|---|---|---|---|
| House Administration | 7 | 4 | 25 | 217 | 266 |
| Interstate & Foreign Commerce | 10 | 45 | 42 | 112 | 154 |
| Banking | 4 | 14 | 50 | 85 | 149 |
| Appropriations | 29 | 59 | 71 | 98 | 131 |
| Education & Labor | 10 | 25 | 77 | 114 | 120 |
| Ways & Means | 12 | 22 | 24 | 63 | 94 |
| Merchant Marine & Fisheries | 6 | 9 | 21 | 28 | 91 |
| Interior | 4 | 10 | 14 | 57 | 87 |
| Science & Technology | — | 17 | 26 | 47 | 87 |
| Government Operations | 9 | 54 | 60 | 68 | 86 |
| Budget | — | — | — | 67 | 84 |
| International Relations | 10 | 14 | 21 | 54 | 83 |
| Judiciary | 7 | 27 | 35 | 69 | 82 |
| Public Works | 6 | 32 | 40 | 88 | 82 |
| Agriculture | 9 | 10 | 17 | 48 | 71 |
| Post Office & Civil Service | 6 | 9 | 46 | 61 | 66 |
| Small Business | — | — | — | 27 | 49 |
| Armed Services | 10 | 15 | 37 | 38 | 47 |
| Rules | 4 | 2 | 7 | 18 | 42 |
| District of Columbia | 7 | 8 | 15 | 43 | 39 |
| Veterans Affairs | 7 | 18 | 18 | 26 | 33 |
| Standards of Official Conduct | — | — | 5 | 5 | 16 |
| Internal Security | 10 | 46 | 51 | 27 | — |

## TABLE 2b

## STAFF SIZE OF SENATE COMMITTEES, SELECTED YEARS

| Senate Committees | 1947 | 1960 | 1970 | 1975 | 1979 |
|---|---|---|---|---|---|
| Judiciary | 19 | 137 | 190 | 251 | 172 |
| Governmental Affairs | 29 | 47 | 55 | 144 | 162 |
| Labor & Human Resources | 9 | 28 | 69 | 150 | 120 |
| Commerce, Science & Transportation | 8 | 52 | 53 | 111 | 88 |
| Budget | — | — | — | 90 | 82 |
| Appropriations | 23 | 31 | 42 | 72 | 80 |
| Environment (Public Works) | 10 | 11 | 34 | 70 | 72 |
| Foreign Relations | 8 | 25 | 31 | 62 | 68 |
| Energy & Natural Resources (Interior) | 7 | 26 | 22 | 53 | 55 |
| Banking, Housing & Urban Affairs | 9 | 22 | 23 | 55 | 46 |
| Finance | 6 | 6 | 16 | 26 | 41 |
| Agriculture, Nutrition & Forestry | 3 | 10 | 7 | 22 | 31 |
| Rules & Administration | 41 | 15 | 13 | 29 | 31 |
| Armed Services | 10 | 23 | 19 | 30 | 27 |
| Veterans Affairs | — | — | — | 32 | 23 |
| Aeronautics & Space Science | — | 10 | 12 | 22 | — |
| District of Columbia | 4 | 7 | 12 | 22 | — |
| Post Office & Civil Service | 46 | 20 | 31 | 25 | — |

# PRESIDENTIAL-CONGRESSIONAL RELATIONS IN THE 1980s

Harvey C. Mansfield, Sr.
Columbia University

Perhaps it is well to begin by rejecting one apparent possibility which, if it should materialize, would be symptomatic of a major change in the working nature of our constitutional regime, reversing trends of the past seven decades.

In the 20 years since 1960 no president has succeeded in serving out the two full terms that the 22nd Amendment allows; only two were twice nominated and only one, Nixon, re-elected. During that period also the appointive vice-presidency introduced by the 25th Amendment (making virtually obsolete the unrepealed succession statute) came into operation twice. And during much of the period a Republican president confronted a Democratic Congress. These circumstances were partly matters of chance. Nevertheless, in the aftermath of President Carter's administration and the very substantial concomitant and relevant transformation of congressional institutions, they made it pertinent to ask a preliminary question. Are the 1980s, in some reversion to 19th-Century precedents, likely to become an era of one-term presidencies?

It is only a half-truth and not a truism of American politics that all roads lead ultimately to the Congress. The weight of historical evidence still appears to support the dictum (as Hamilton argued) that the prospect of a second term is good for both the presidency and the congress—for the continuing vitality, that is, of the separation of powers. Renomination for President Carter presented a fair test case; his second candidacy met a notable lack of public and press enthusiasm. When the rival challenge finally came in the fall of 1979, Senator Kennedy was widely thought capable of sweeping Carter aside; yet the event proved otherwise.

In the perspective of mid-1981 the specific question can apparently be answered in the negative. Once again, as Taft, Hoover and Truman had shown earlier in this century, and Ford more recently, the resources and advantages of an incumbent president, even when beset by adversity—let alone when riding high, like Johnson in 1964 and Nixon in 1972—are enough to frustrate a formidable challenge within the President's party. Control of his renomination, whatever the outcome in November, should be enough to preserve the two-term expectation from atrophy.

Another consideration argues that a one-term era would not in any event signal a return to the past. The ubiquitous media and the relentless round of primaries leave no room for the 19th-Century degree of congressional influence on the nominating processes. Although the challenge to Carter came from a senator, the issues between them did not turn on congressional prerogatives. If in 1984 or later another outsider, Governor Brown of California for instance, proves able with the help of federal campaign funds to capture the Democratic nomination as Carter did in 1976, or should former Congressman John Anderson, say, take the Republican succession away from Reagan, it will not be the result of a congressional cabal. Proposed reforms of the primary system do not point in the direction of greater congressional controls over the outcome.

Some major trends, nevertheless, institutional and other, existing or in plain sight, and mostly seeming irreversible forecast durable effects on the conduct of business between the two ends of Pennsylvania Avenue—effects sufficient to distinguish the 1970s from the 1980s. Four of these warrant mention. With one exception their near-term impacts suggest differences in degree more than in kind, continuation of current trends. Their ultimate consequences may be something else if critical tipping points are reached.

### Institutional Trends

First, and already in place, are the changes over the last two decades in the attitudes and behavior of members of Congress—and especially in the House where the consequences are most strikingly in evidence. James Sundquist has labelled these the "new individualism" and the "new assertiveness."[1] The days of autocracy in the leadership, chamber-wide, ended with the rebellion against Speaker Cannon in 1910, and the downfall of Senator Nelson Aldrich. The subsequent dominance, over the next sixty years or so, of an oligarchy of committee chairman—a dozen in the Senate, a score in the House—entrenched by the seniority rule, has in turn been undermined.[2] Sundquist dates the turning point from the elections of 1958, which brought to both houses, a "critical mass" of newcomers, products of direct primaries from constituencies where local party discipline had crumbled or a new independent style had developed, and candidates were pretty much on their own in obtaining their nominations and elections. Individualists, not the party's faithful, came into office by this route, and they proceeded to behave as individualists in office. Any single date would be arbitrary; over the ensuing fifteen or twenty years the oligarchs lost their separate empires and were supplanted, one by one. Organizational changes responded to the new generation's needs.

House committee chairmen came to be named by secret caucus ballot, and their powers over subcommittees, staff assignments, agenda and scheduling were severely trimmed. The number of subcommittees approached 150 in both chambers. Each subcommittee got its own staff and expense allowance. Half the House Democrats could be subcommittee chairman, and every Republican a ranking minority member. Senate Democrats averaged two subcommittee chairmanships apiece. Until 1975, at least, turnover rates in office decreased and average tenure increased to unprecedented lengths. Legislative jurisdiction became so splintered that any matter of substance attracting, or likely to attract, notice in the media was subject to the rival claims of half a dozen or more subcommittees. Essentially, each subcommittee chairman

---

[1] See his paper, "The Separation of Powers: An Old Dilemma in a New Age," presented at the Center for the Study of Democratic Politics, University of Pennsylvania, Philadelphia, Pa., November 28–29, 1979. *Cf.* my chapter, "The Dispersion of Authority in Congress," in H. C. Mansfield, Sr., ed., *Congress Against the President* (New York: Praeger, 1975). These developments have been widely noticed by Congress-watchers. Anthony King uses the term "atomization" in *The New American Political System* (Washington, D.C.: American Enterprise Institute, 1978), pp. 388–395.

[2] The proliferation of subcommittees and erosion of chairmen's powers are ironic testimony to the frailty of predictions of the consequences of structural modifications. George Galloway, the political scientist who, as staff adviser to the LaFollette-Monroney committee, largely fashioned the Legislative Reorganization Act of 1946, was probably as knowledgeable an observer of congressional affairs as could then have been found. The Act envisaged a limited number of strong committees.

with a bit of jurisdictional turf and a careerist outlook had the resources and incentives to go into some fraction of the public's business on his own.

Turnover in both chambers has risen markedly in the 1974 and subsequent elections, from the comparative stability of the previous two decades, though it is not high by earlier historical standards. In the 94th, 95th, 96th and 97th Congresses (1974, 1976, 1978 and 1980 elections) the percentages of newcomers in the Senate were, respectively, 11, 18, 20 and 18; and in the House 21, 15, 17 and 17. Individual complaints of frustration are heard as voluntary retirements are announced; perhaps the new conditions of congressional life are not so rewarding after all, since the harassments of single-issue groups and district-office case work have grown so burdensome.

A consequence in 1980, in the second session of the 96th, was that half of the senators (49%) and somewhat over half the representatives (53%) had not yet served six years in office—the threshold requirement for members to qualify for congressional pensions. In the first session of the 97th the comparable proportions were 55% for the Senate and 46% for the House. With experience in short supply in both the legislative and executive branches, the problems of communications and cooperation magnified.

Second, and closely connected with the first, is the great expansion of congressional staff help, perquisites and logistic facilities. Things have come a long way since Lindsay Rogers, giving possibly the earliest systematic academic attention to the topic forty years ago, could conclude that it would be well if committee clerks were more expert, but he foresaw "great difficulty" if they became too expert on such matters as financial or military affairs: "experts would be pitted against experts."[3] During the years since the Legislative Reorganization Act of 1946 first authorized professional staff assistants for all standing committees, to be appointed on the basis of merit, the legislative branch has been the fastest-growing part of the federal civilian establishment, and especially

---

[3] "The Staffing of Congress," *PSQ* 56 (March 1941), 1. "The extreme situation would probably result if the Naval and Military Affairs Committees had their own soldiers and sailors as experts." *Ibid.* at pp. 21–22.

so during the 1970s.[4] The growth has been across the board; committee staff, subcommittee staff, minority staff, members' staff both office and district, party leadership (minority s well as majority), steering and policy committee staff, direct support staff, such as the Office of Legislative Counsel and the new Congressional Budget Office, and supporting agencies, the GAO, the Library of Congress and its Congressional Research Service, the newer Office of Technology Assessment, the Government Printing Office, Architect of the Capitol, buildings and grounds, police, and so on.

The combined committee staffs of both chambers totalled 483 authorized positions in 1947 and 3,082 employees in 1976. Members' personal staffs totalled 2,030 in 1947 and 10,190 in 1976. For the legislative branch as a whole the increase was from 25, 669 in 1947 to 38,870 in 1976.[5] The dollar comparisons are more spectacular. The legislative branch as a whole expended $40 million in 1947, $165 million by 1965, and $1.077 billion in 1979. The budget estimate for 1980 was up another 33 percent, to $1.331 billion.[6] As members' salaries have multiplied six times over from

---

[4] This comparative assertion is based on numbers of employees directly on federal payrolls. The executive branch totalled 2,075,000 in 1949 and an estimated 2,803,000 in 1979; the peak, 2,980,000, occurred in 1969 (*Special Analyses, Budget of the U.S. Government, Fiscal Year 1979* [Washington, D.C.: G.P.O., 1978], p. 210). The *Budget, Fiscal Year 1981*, Summary Table 8, p. 558, gives a figure of 1,893,391 for 1979 year-end full-time permanent employees, excluding the Postal Service and other off-Budget agencies.

Full-time permanent federal employment has been subject to annual ceilings, reviewed with the budget since the LBJ administration, in a perverse and popular misuse of budgeting principles. The Civil Service Reform Act of 1978, sec. 311, limited year-end full-time employment for fiscal years 1979, 1980 and 1981 to the total count on September 30, 1977; in case of need, the president can increase it by no more than the proportionate increase in the whole population of the country.

If it were possible to segregate and count separately all employees paid partly or wholly with federal funds, on the rolls of federal contractors, subcontractors, grantees, state, local and foreign governments (with revenue-sharing and foreign-aid funds)—not to speak of recipients of various categories of benefit-payment transfers (unemployment compensation, Social Security, Medicare, welfare, food stamps, etc.) different comparisons might be made. Total annual federal outlays over the past 30 years have multiplied perhaps as much as fifteen times over, depending on what and how things are counted.

[5] Harrison W. Fox, Jr., and Susan Hammond, *Congressional Staffs* (New York: Free Press, 1977), Appendix Table 1, p. 168 and Table 3, p. 171; Census Bureau, *Historical Statistics, Colonial Times to 1957*, p. 710, col. 249. There is a delusive exactitude about these numbers, depending on the sources and definitions the compilers used. Somewhat smaller numbers, running through 1978 and broken down in greater detail, are contained in the *Final Report of the House Select Committee on Committees*, H. Rept. no. 96-866, 96th Cong., 2d sess. (April 1, 1980).

[6] Congressional Quarterly, *Congress and the Nation, 1945–1964* (Washington, D.C., 1965), p. 1418; *Budget of the United States, Fiscal Year 1967*, Summary Table 5, p. 43 and Pt. 5, pp. 166-178 (Legislative Branch); *U.S. Budget Appendix, Fiscal Year 1981*, H. Doc 96-247, Pt. 8, pp. 373–382.

the annual figure of $10,000 at the end of World War II, so staff salaries, retirement benefits and other perquisites, office space, travel and other expense allowances have expanded correspondingly. An increase in any of these categories is an argument for increase in the others.

A more useful indicator of congressional staff expansion might be the pages or linear feet of shelves of printed committee and subcommittee hearings—a reflection *par excellence* of staff work. I have no doubt that this indicator would confirm the others; but my efforts to quantify here were frustrated by the fact that librarians now put these materials on microfilm.

Yet the vast increase in staff and staff work has not been associated with increase of legislation passed by Congress. The remarkable stability of legislative output over the years before and during congressional staff expansion (with the alternating rhythm from first to second sessions) contrasts sharply with the surging output of executive agencies (see Table I). The apparently limitless capacity of executive agency staffs to generate more law out of increasingly extended and complicated statutory delegations, with their restraining provisos, has not been matched by the capacity of congressional staffs to make Congress more productive of policies that require action by the legislature as a whole. But a turning of the regulatory tide in the Reagan administration brought some reduction in Federal Register pages in 1981. The reduction in congressional output was far sharper: only eleven pages of public laws enacted in the first three months of the 97th Congress, and only 145 laws that year, although the 576-page Omnibus Budget Reconciliation Act redressed the imbalance of words.

The chief significance of congressional staff growth is the new capability and motivation it introduces on the congressional side of relationships with the presidency and, more generally, with the executive branch. The capability is twofold. Partly it is for sustained and technical investigation and criticism across the range of agencies and issues, more or less simultaneously, and less rather than more concertedly. Partly it is for the formulation and technical elaboration of a variety of often inconsistent alternatives to any executive proposal. The executive is no longer in possession of the only available working draft. In varying degrees, experts are pitted against experts.

The new motivation is to exploit these capabilities to the fullest, in the interests not only of members but also of the new legions of staff people. They enjoy many advantages but not tenure.

Their career incentives accordingly put a premium on activity and expansion.

Taken together, the new breed of legislators, the newly democratized relations among them, and the greatly enhanced staff and facilities at their disposal, required alterations in previous patterns of executive-congressional relations. The 93rd Congress (1973–74) staked out far-reaching claims in furtherance of congressional prerogatives designed to insure a break with past practices. Both houses instructed their committees to place more emphasis on the oversight of administrative performances. The War Powers Resolution, the Congressional Budget and Impoundment Control Act, the requirement that the Attorney General appoint a special prosecutor (whose independence is protected by statute) to handle cases of alleged improbity of high executive officials, the exposure of the CIA and the FBI, and the Freedom of Information Act Amendments, along with the Supreme Court's decision rejecting Nixon's unqualified claim of executive privilege for White House papers and testimony, have tilted the balance of power away from the President.

The 1980s will test the limits and durability of these legislative assertions. The 1981 session opened with a slaughter of Democratic staffers on the Senate side, and there were pressures to reduce the legislative budget along with the executive. But in the longer term it seems doubtful that Republican legislators, when they are in the majority, will want to get along with less help than Democratic majorities allowed.

In the late 1970s, congressional activism was aimed mainly at the departments and agencies, rather than at the president or his office. Failure to respond to the president was more common than direct assault. There are exceptions and these may be important. The Bert Lance affair, for example, distracted Carter's attention from urgent business for crucial weeks in 1977 and cost him the services of a man he valued highly. But more characteristically the burdens piling up on the presidency have been what Neustadt calls "clerkship" functions thrust up to his office as direct or indirect consequences of congressional mandates to others.

Industrious committee oversight, for instance, may raise issues of executive confidentiality that need White House attention. The legislative veto, long a rarity viewed with suspicion in some congressional quarters after its introduction in the Reorganization Act of 1939 where it was a means of increasing presidential discretion, has lately become a great congressional favorite. Now that it wears the garb of increased congressional control, it has been included in scores of different types of legislation. In practice, much of its value is symbolic: apart from reorganization plans, the veto has been exercised in only a handful of relatively sensitive cases—e.g., Federal Election Commission regulations of campaign funds; GSA regulations for the custody of Nixon's papers—out of some hundreds of minatory statutory provisions for it.[7] Varied combinations of the component procedural elements of veto provisions by both houses, by either house alone, by inaction or by a positive vote before a specified deadline, by a majority vote or two-thirds, etc. are White House concerns both as bargaining chips and as precedents.

"Sunset" provisions, fixing terminal dates for the organic acts of executive agencies unless specifically extended, and the practice of requiring annual authorizing legislation before appropriations are in order, are two other means currently in favor for selectively exerting congressional controls. Both are calculated to enhance the strength of the legislative committees and to embroil the presidency in labors of mediation that bring little political reward unless in the form of an improved reputation for skill.

Still another strategy for imposing congressional restraints on the executive branch is to set up additional agencies or procedures to monitor agency performance, thereby supplying grist for the mills of congressional committees and staffs. This supplies opportunities, too, for needling the president as to who "shall take care that the laws be faithfully executed." The GAO is the leading example; its scope and authority greatly increased during the 1970s. The Environmental Protection Agency and its Act, the Equal Employment Opportunity Commission and the Merit Systems Protection Board are also examples.

*Demographic Trends*

A third significant trend in the 1980s has direct political consequences for the president's relations with Congress because it redefines the constituencies of both. The 1980 census confirmed and extended two sorts of shifts in the country's population and

---

[7] See *Studies on the Legislative Veto* prepared by the Congressional Research Service for the Subcommittee on House Rules, committee print, House Rules Committee, 96th Congress, 2d session, (February 1980).

wealth, shifts long under way which will get explicit constitutional and statutory recognition for the ensuing decade. One has to do with location, the other with composition. Both substantially affect political interests.

The continuing movement of people from the northeastern and upper midwestern states to the south, southwest and Pacific coast necessitates a reapportionment of nearly all House seats, effective with the 1982 elections. The Census Bureau's certification to Congress showed gains of three seats each for Florida and for Texas, two for California and one each for Connecticut, Tennessee and a half dozen Rocky Mountain, desert and northwest states, from New Mexico to Washington—sixteen altogether. The prospective losers are New York, down five; Pennsylvania, Ohio and Illinois, two each; and Massachusetts, Missouri, Michigan, New Jersey and South Dakota, one each. These are incremental changes, directly involving only three percent of the House seats and ten gainers and eight losers among the fifty states. But the gap between the California and New York delegations, the two largest, which was 30 to 43 in the Eisenhower administration, 38 to 41 in the Kennedy-Johnson period and 43 to 39 when Carter was elected in 1976, is due to widen markedly, to 45 to 34 in California's favor. Texas, with 27, moves to third place, ahead of Pennsylvania and Ohio. More important, the intrastate redistricting required not only in these states but elsewhere in order to equalize district populations, will erode the representation of virtually all northern cities, historic strongholds of liberal Democrats. Many hitherto safe Democratic seats will become marginal. For the first time in thirty years a fair prospect of Republican control of the House looms, and with it, of the Congress in 1982. If that should prove to be the outcome it may well reverse the experience of 1954 and last through the decade. The Census Bureau reported on April 12, 1980 51 percent of the voting age population resides in the South and West. Statutory formulas governing the distribution of federal funds for many programs will accordingly swing the flow of money away from the older large cities, where urban, social, and fiscal problems are concentrated, toward suburban and Sun Belt communities tending to make the rich richer and leaving the poor poorer, relatively.

The 1980 census will also reveal more precisely the changing age composition of the population—an increase in the proportion of older people and an increase in the proportion of wealthier people. The South and West have attracted more than their numerical share of young entrepreneurs as well as pensioners and the well-to-do has-beens. Regional banks have exploited the rapid accumulation of investment funds. The political effects of these constituency shifts will not be lost on the presidents and congresses of the 1980s.

## Judicial Activism

In 1952, in the *Steel Seizure Case* the Supreme Court told President Truman that he could not ignore unwelcome or unhelpful acts of Congress and fashion a remedy for crisis more to his liking on the strength of executive authority alone.

In 1954 in the *School Segregation Cases,* the Court started a sequence of events that obliged President Eisenhower, like it or not, to send federal troops to Central High School in Little Rock, Arkansas, and also put on the agenda of Congress for the next two decades the highly controversial issues involved in federal aid, civil rights and school busing.

No comparable judicial intervention marked the Kennedy and Johnson administrations. But in President Nixon's term troubles from that quarter came not in single spies but whole battalions. His first two nominees to the Court were rejected by the Senate; his impoundments of formula fund allocations were enjoined; his papers and tapes, despite pleas of executive privilege, were subjected to subpoenas as evidence in criminal trials, though not in congressional committee investigations; a statute was sustained that declared, contrary to weighty precedent, that these records are public property. These decisions were crucial in presidential-congressional relations.

Presidents Ford and Carter escaped serious judicial entanglements. Historically, Court doctrine, once the reluctance to take jurisdiction has been overcome, has tended to support the president in foreign affairs and the Congress in domestic issues. It is impossible to foresee whether and in what circumstances during the 1980s the two-branch issues may be made triangular. Perhaps a legislative veto case? An extension of judicial review over the spending power or budget processes? Issues of federalism in connection with block grants or water rights? The authority of the President unilaterally to dispose of frozen Iranian assets? Constitutional rights of undocumented aliens, involved in measures to resolve some of the contradictions of immigration policy? These are speculations about issues that might divide the executive and the legislature, or parts thereof.

It does seem likely that the resignation of Justice Potter Stewart provides only the first of several vacancies on the Supreme Court that President Reagan may be called upon to fill, enough perhaps to produce decisive shifts in Court doctrine. It is impossible to foresee the consequences these might have for presidential-congressional relations.

### Freedom of Information and Executive Privilege

During the 1970s the balance tilted against the president and the executive branch also in the matter of controlling the flow of information to Congress, the news media and the public at large. The Freedom of Information Act as amended has made hitherto confidential government files accessible to interested parties and inquiring reporters, access only partly limited by the exempt categories and the protections of the Privacy Act. Communications among high officials have also become subject to revelation to congressional committees as a result of stipulations exacted in the course of Senate confirmation of appointments in cases where executive privilege might be claimed. The exposure of CIA and FBI files and the protections for "whistle-blowers" included in the Civil Service Reform Act of 1978 have salutary aims for the long term, but in the short run create difficulties in maintaining discipline. The precedent in the original Atomic Energy Act of 1947, requiring the AEC to keep the Joint Committee on Atomic Energy "fully and currently informed" (including copies of budget "green sheets") has been extended in modified forms by the War Powers Resolution of 1973 and other statutes to a wider range of agencies.

The old maxim that forewarned is forearmed helps the president's opponents. It would not be a popular campaign for him to take head-on a plea for more privacy for executive deliberations, but it seems likely that presidents in the 1980s will do what they can to tilt the balance back in that direction.

### Policy Areas

In a look for salient issues of policy a decade ahead, the foreground is inevitably foreshortened. In 1970 who talked of oil shortages or the overthrow of the Shah? In 1980 the campuses were quiet and Spiro Agnew and George Wallace forgotten. Yet some intractable issues spanned the decade. At least three of them seem sure to confront the Presidents and Congress throughout the 1980s.

First, the complexities and contradictions of energy policy have divided Congress and set it against the President ever since Carter's inauguration. Considering the very modest progress toward firm legislative policy in this field achieved in 1980 after three years of contention together with the pace and scale of new investment required for massive shifts in energy sources, it seems safe to list this subject high among the policy concerns for the foreseeable future.

Second, the twin faces of domestic economic trouble, inflation and unemployment, promise to plague the decade of the 1980s. In the mid-1960s Walter Heller, then Chairman of the Council of Economic Advisers, persuaded Presidents Kennedy and Johnson that a substantial tax cut in the face of a budget deficit would both stimulate the economy and yield higher revenues, a prediction vindicated in the short run after the 1964 tax act. Reviewing that experience, he later expressed the beliefs and aspirations of a respectable school of economists that their science had so far advanced as to be capable, given political support, of prescribing and "fine-tuning" a correct fiscal policy.[8] Vietnam and its aftermath shattered that confidence. OPEC introduced massive new inflationary forces that confound economic advisers.

The 1980s opened with drastic measures by the Federal Reserve to control the money supply and by the President and Congress toward budget-balancing. No evident consensus, among economists or politicians, marked the proper course of action should these measures fail in their purpose or entail side effects as bad as the conditions they were supposed to remedy. In particular, the harmony temporarily prevailing early in 1981 among the three centers of authority, the Federal Reserve, the Congress and the President, would be subject to differential strains from their different constituencies.

---

[8] Walter W. Heller, *New Dimensions of Political Economy* (Cambridge, Mass.: Harvard University Press, 1966).

The Federal Reserve, more than the other two, is responsive to considerations of international finance, exchange rates, the interests of money market banks abroad and, along with the Treasury, of the international lending agencies. Not since 1920 has it seemed so directly the author of painful domestic austerity. If it becomes a scapegoat, can it count on firm presidential-congressional support to ward off the fate that befell two other postwar symbols of power, secrecy and independence, the CIA and the FBI?

As for the president and Congress, the disruptive effects of inflation and unemployment will aggravate what John Gardner has called "the war of the parts against the whole," and test the efficacy of the new regime of congressional budgeting. However, President Reagan's staff may have discovered, in the "budget reconciliation" resolution introduced in the 1974 Congressional Budget Act, a potent new instrument for imposing a centralized fiscal control.

Third, the overriding issues of foreign policy will test the settlement that the 93rd Congress imposed on the presidency after Vietnam. The Carter administration scored impressive achievements in securing the ratification of the Panama Canal treaty and the accord between Egypt and Israel. But detente and arms control and the reconciliation of Israeli, Palestinian and Persian Gulf interests are as much the unfinished business of the 1980s as they were of the 1970s. An arms race looms. Iran and other unstable elements in the mid-east have supplanted Southeast Asia as the focus of concerns that are unlikely to be allayed any more quickly. The amelioration of economic and social conditions in the southern hemisphere, African and Latin American, will be on the national agenda at the end of the 1980s as it is at the beginning, and so, too, more generally, will be the governance of international commerce and investment and the development of oceanic resources. The whole spectrum of possible presidential-congressional relationships is sooner or later exhibited in the conduct of foreign policy.

None of these three bundles of issues fits comfortably into Theodore Lowi's neat conceptual categories of policy types—distributive, regulatory and redistributive—with their attendant predictions of correlative types of politics, patronage, interest group and class. Presidents and congresses will muddle their way through, Lindblom-fashion, to such policy resolutions as they can manage.

## Patterns of Conflict, Consensus and Cooperation

In the general context sketched above, what can usefully be hazarded about presidential-congressional relations in the 1980s? Observations on nine topics follow, touching (1) the durability of the separation of shared powers, and the enhanced need for informal understandings to secure inter-branch cooperation; (2) the aggravations of divided party control; (3) the overburdened presidency; (4) the overburdened Congress; (5) incentives toward inter-branch cooperation; (6) consequences for the president of the dispersion of authority in Congress; (7) prospects of an all-Republican national government; (8) strategies for the president; and (9) government from a bomb shelter.

*First,* although revolutions almost by definition are unpredictable, (they may appear otherwise in hindsight) *nothing in prospect points to fundamental alterations in the two branches, of a sort that involve a constitutional amendment.* Perennial suggestions are heard for introducing features of parliamentary regimes, such as relaxing the ban against dual office-holding, but none has organized support. The separation of shared powers is as firmly in place as ever, and with it the potentialities of confrontation and stalemate and the consequent necessity of informal, extra-legal methods of cooperation in getting things done. Some of these may become institutionalized, as for example the congressional liaison staff in the White House.

The interdependence of the presidency and Congress is markedly greater since the 20th Amendment converted the jobs of most congressmen from part-time to full-time employment. It has become greater also since congressional legislation has come to cover nearly all aspects of our lives. The former circumstance leaves no respite for the president; the latter, no respite for the legislators.

Prior to the 20th Amendment, an incoming president had nine months of his first year in office to get his new administration in presentable shape before the Congress descended on him as a body. He had also six months or so of each succeeding year to consider whether he regarded the presence or the absence of Congress as the greater blessing. He could always call a special session if needed, but the latter option seemed preferable if he could make do with the laws and funds already in hand. The main rationale of the Amendment was that it would do away with the biennial "lame-duck" sessions and the opportunities for irresponsible filibustering tactics and other abuses they afforded. A secondary rationale was that the new Congress, sworn in two or three weeks before the inaugural date, provided the proper forum for promptly settling the presidential election if the Electoral College returns were inconclusive. This contingency has not yet arisen, but instead an unanticipated consequence has emerged. When the new president arrives, still breathless from his campaign, the Congress and its commitees are organized and ready to pounce on him.[9] From then on, they are omnipresent; and, indeed, the President could not now do without them, since funds and authorizations are kept on a short leash. So the premium on cooperation is higher, while the opportunities for confrontation are at the same time magnified.

*Second,* on the record of the past 30 years, *the odds are about even that a Republican will be elected president while Democrats retain control of one or both houses of Congress.* The presidential selection process, a multitude of primaries and caucuses, public financing of campaigns, and TV campaigning, all tend to detach the candidates from party organizations, platforms and discipline. All of this caters to "independent" voters and to votes based on the candidate's personality appeal. Divided party control need not lead to confrontations such as Nixon provoked, but it inevitably adds the complications of partisan rivalry to the processes of cooperation. It puts a premium on protocol in communications between the branches.

The record of the past 30 years, as has been noted at an earlier point, may be no reliable guide if the Republicans should win control of both houses as well as the presidency. But an all-Republican government, like an all-Democratic one must cope with similar factional rivalries, differently weighted, based on ideology, interests and geography, Conservative Democrats may be courted to offset liberal Republican defectors.

*Third, the presidency is plainly overburdened,* as much as it was in 1937 when FDR echoed the report of the Brownlow Commitee,

---

[9] See the discussion in ch. 11, "Hazards of Transition" in the third edition of Richard E. Neustadt, *Presidential Power: The Politics of Leadership from FDR to Carter* (New York: Wiley, 1980).

that "the President needs help." The White House staff that evolved in response to that diagnosis seems in turn to have been overrun, choked with business. It is an old marketing principle that a quantum increase in productive capacity for something that customers want will draw a corresponding increase in demand. The attention of the White House is a commodity much in demand. The existence of the White House staff, of the Executive Office of the President, and of National Security Council staff, has unquestionably exerted a strong centralizing tendency on policy deliberations within the executive branch. For three decades this contributed to the lead the presidency held in dealings with Congress. That lead is no longer apparent. But there is a heavy central accumulation of clerkship functions and departmental affairs. Much of it involves congressional relations.[10] A larger White House staff makes the presidency more accessible to legislators with axes to grind and visions to promote.

It is tempting to urge presidents to divest their offices of most of this traffic, to husband their resources for a limited and selected number of "important" issues which by control of timing and tactics they can hope to influence decisively. It is brave counsel. The trick is in the doing. Presidents on occasion share with other people impulses of a friendly or dutiful nature to be helpful to others when they can be; they cannot always be protected against distractions. Apart from such stray impulses, two sorts of more systematic considerations, militate against following the advice. The importance of an issue is not always intrinsic but is often dependent on who is involoved; trivial things may matter if they concern important people. And in the bargaining that necessarily attends the exercise of presidential leadership, all sorts of matters otherwise unrelated may become important if they are tied together in a deal. It is seldom possible to settle a single issue in isolation, exclusively on its particular merits.

---

[10] While browsing in the White House files in the LBJ Library, Austin, Texas, I came on a staff memo of February 28, 1966 from Harry C. McPherson, Jr., for the President, reporting a controversy over the price of milk in the midwest. Wilbur Mills and Speaker Carl Albert were "adamant" in demanding that Secretary of Agriculture Orville Freeman prevent a scheduled seasonal drop in wholesale milk prices, as the marketing orders required. What to do? A penciled marginal note in LBJ's hand reads, "Get Pres. out of this." WHCF Executive Cn/Milk BE5–2.

More positively, an open Congress is an invitation to the president to infiltrate its membership and cultivate organized support inside it for his measures. Perhaps paradoxically, this seems to require a substantial buildup in his congressional liaison staff. Such a strategy of presidential influence depends heavily on the incumbent's ability to develop a reputation for professional political skills among an audience of professional politicians.

An alternative strategy of presidential influence is indirect, reflected on legislators through their constituents. As Neustadt has argued,[11] it consists in cultivating his prestige and promoting his programs through informal sessions with groups of opinion leaders and their spokesmen, and by exploiting the media, especially TV. The media, too, have their own interests in exploiting him. Since Kennedy we have not had in the office an easy and graceful master of the TV and its potentialities until Reagan's inauguration. He may make it a hallmark of presidential influence in the 1980s.

*Fourth, the Congress is also overburdened,* collectively in its two chambers, and individually. More information and misinformation comes in than can humanly be absorbed, more claims for attention or action than can be attended to. Democratized in organization and splintered in interests, the members are vulnerable to the demands of single interest groups. The organs of its governance—the authority of the leadership, the caucus and policy committees—are in an inchoate state. It is problematical whether in the 1980s the members will choose to strengthen these organs in order to increase their institutional capacity to determine the course of national policy, or to leave them weak in deference to, or tolerance of, the pursuit of members' individual interests. The former course lends itself more readily to systematic and routinized dealings with the president, as adversary or ally; the latter is adapted to detailed oversight of bureaus and agencies and guerrilla tactics.

*Fifth, the intercameral and inter-branch consensus necessary to consummate legislation, or to give firm support to the president in a course of action already within his formal powers, may simply fail to materialize,* or may be postponed for extended periods, even—or especially— on matters of great moment. *If a sufficient consensus is to form, no single route or strategy leads surely to that result.*

---

[11] *Op. cit.,* chs. 4 and 5, on "Professional Reputation" and "Public Prestige."

But some favoring circumstances can be specified. One is a quick and near-unanimous sentiment arising in response to a dramatically visible external event. Thus in 1941 Pearl Harbor resolved overnight the arguments of three years over defense and foreign policy. Thus the appearance of an inflationary 20 percent prime interest rate in March 1980 briefly induced the Congress in May to insist on a balance, for the first time in years, in its 1981 Budget Resolution. The president cannot manufacture such an event; the consensus itself may not last longer than second thoughts. But he may, with a shrewd sense of timing, capitalize on the event when it occurs. He may, indeed, later manipulate the response to the event, as LBJ was accused of doing with the Gulf of Tonkin Resolution. This method of proceeding by consensus is *ad hoc* unless the sentiment becomes an automatic response to a repetitive type of event. So disaster relief for losses from tornadoes and hurricanes became a regularized routine. The 1980s may well bring more legislation by that method, in immigration policy for instance.

Consensus in initial response to an emergency is characteristically bipartisan. For the first time since the congressional budget procedure came into operation, the May 1980 Budget Resolution for 1981—a conservative fiscal move—was consciously constructed by and for a fragile bipartisan coalition in both Houses in close collaboration with Carter's staff. But it was too fragile to withstand the strains of a campaign year. A counter combination, also bipartisan, of both ends against the middle, defeated it. The sense of urgency then dwindled and the consensus disintegrated. With minor modifications the resolution was finally passed, a month later, by a partisan Democratic majority. A year later, however, the continuance of record-high interest rates and the great reinforcement of Republican and conservative Democratic votes renewed the sense of urgency. This time the bipartisan coalition prevailed in the passage of the 1981 Budget Resolution.

A more durable method of reaching consensus depends on institutionalizing communications and consultation between the White House and Congress. "Durable" is perhaps not an apt term, since on the record of the past three decades presidential liaison must be built afresh by each new incumbent. It is tempting to propose joint presidential-congressional councils for the purpose, but the experience of joint congressional committees and mixed executive-congressional commissions runs to the contrary. Consultation is essential, and task forces, liaison representatives, drafting committees and the like are appropriate to that end. But if the separation of shared powers is to be regularly bridged for legislative objectives, the policy products must emerge from the deliberatons of a group more resembling a council of ambassadors—each needing the concurrence of his principal—than a committee determining its actions by a preponderance of votes. Presidential-congressional relations in the 1980s will continue to be governed by the exigencies of that basic constitutional principle.

*Sixth, the values of cooperation and the prices of getting it are heightened by the dispersion of authority in Congress.* With the erosion of party ties of loyalty and discipline, success for the president at the polls or in his legislative initiatives has become less and less important for the careers of more and more members of Congress who wear the same party badge as his. In a wide range of activities they can do without him. They have found that formula statutes governing how federal benefits are parceled out among states and other recipients greatly reduce the president's ability to use benefits as patronage, to be given or withheld as a means of building and sustaining party organizations in Congress and in the country that might be useful to him. This is one reason for a frequent preference of presidents, when new programs are to be undertaken, for the creation of new agencies not yet shackled in formulas, that at least temporarily augment the supply of discretionary benefits at the disposal of the White House.

With respect to their own leadership, members have moved toward legislating on the floor, by way of amendments offered there, rather than settling disputes in committee and presenting a united front in defense of commitee actions; hence a great increase in the number of formal rollcalls. Moreover, the distribution of individual perquisites inside Congress has been largely routinized in formulas, replacing an intricate system of rewards and punishments at the leadership's disposal with a system more nearly of entitlements that lacks effective sanctions against members if they stay clear of the Ethics Committee and the criminal law.

Instead of party cohesion as a guide, members make their ways amongst the rival claims of a host of single-issue groups, which have been brought into existence, or greatly strengthened by the dramatic enlargement of the public agenda since the impetus of the Johnson administration in domestic affairs. The American Association of Retired Persons (AARP) is a conspicuous example. The result is a seeming paradox: the more active the single-issue activists become, the more passive or indifferent is the voters' response on election day. Turnout, measured by the participation of eligible voters in recent years has dropped to historically low levels. Without the stimulation of strong local party organizations capable of bringing out a large enough vote to afford a generalized support and protection against extremist demands, elected representatives have less incentive to become consistently dependable allies of the president.

*Seventh, the advent of the Reagan administration* and its drive to turn back the legislative and spending programs of the previous fifteen years, and particularly the Republican success in gaining control of the Senate in 1980, along with an arguable prospect of duplicating that success in the House in 1982, *requires reconsideration of trends called "irreversible" earlier in this paper.* Is the "new individualism" perhaps only a phenomenon of Democratic congresses? Will the 1980 and 1982 elections prove to be "critical elections," in the sense of marking a lasting realignment of party affiliations that may lock in Republican control of the national government for the next two decades or more? It remains to be seen whether Republican congressional behavior will differ from the Democratic pattern, now that their party controls the White House.

In the 1980 campaign William Brock, the Republican National Committee's chairman, concentrated attention and resources on congressional and state and local races.[12] Press reports indicate that the Committee's fund-raising capacity, surpassing previous experience, was such that virtually every successful Republican member of the House in 1981 had received more financial support from the Committee than from any other source; and that Brock had been at pains to see that this was so. By contrast, Democratic candidates, as in the past, were on their own—the National Committee concentrating on Carter's campaign—and so, were more vulnerable to single issue groups with money to spend, pro or

---

[12] *New York Times,* Jan. 18, 1981, p. 18; Jan. 26, 1981, p.22; *Congressional Quarterly Weekly Report,* Vol. 39, no. 4 (Jan. 24, 1981), p. 201.

con. If the Republican National Committee should thereby become a major factor in enabling that pary to win control of the House as well as the Senate in 1982 and thereafter, the basis may be laid for a resurgence of party discipline on their side of the aisle for the remainder of the decade, and for a much closer set of ties between the president and Congress.

It is necessary to go back to the Harding-Coolidge-Hoover era to find a sustained period of Republican control of both branches, a period too long ago for confident comparisons, beyond the observation that presidents did not dominate congresses in those days. No one could wish for a repetition of the events that brought that era to a close.

*Eighth, no single strategy for securing interbranch cooparation can be prescribed.* The 1980s open an era in which many features of the old party politics, lamented or envied, will not work, for the 1970s brought systemic changes.

Some guidelines toward cooperative relationships can be suggested. In general, since the Congress regards oversight as its function and has equipped itself accordingly, the president probably has more to lose than to gain by disputing every inch of that ground. Bearing in mind the difficulties and temptations noted earlier, let him nevertheless try to distance himself from most clashes of economic interest groups, bureaucratic jurisdictional rivalries and competing technical claims, and conserve his resources for selective intervention when he sees an important principle or national interest at stake.

Let the president actively cultivate good congressional relations as a healthy end in itself and not only as an instrument for getting his own way more frequently. To this end a liaison staff skilled in congressional politics and not merely schooled in executive desires is needed. To this end also it should usually be helpful to recognize the congressional leadership in seeking cooperation, rather than bypass it; and beyond that, to identify and try to work with members whose orientation is toward the institution of which they are parts. On principles of comity a wholesume respect for the Congress as an institution is appropriate for a president who hopes for a reciprocal regard for his office. A symbiotic relationship is possible and constructive.

It is an aspiration, not a guideline, to look for the day when a natural political leader has the opportunity, the talent and the wit to exploit effectively the resources of TV for direct access to the voters, and in doing so succeeds, in not only winning the presidency, but also in carrying with him a substantial majority for his party in Congress—members thereby in some degree consciously beholden to him. That will be a good day for cooperation and not a bad day for the congressional reforms of the past two decades either. But television is so much a vehicle for entertainment, whatever information and enlightenment it also provides, that this prospect is only a possibility, not something to be counted upon.

Cooperation between the president and Congress, for all that can be said for its virtues and benefits, is not an absolute imperative, an inherent good for all occasions and purposes. Times will come in the 1980s as they have in the past when one constitutional partner or the other turns instead to confrontation as the more desirable or necessary. The Constitution gives weapons to each, specifically for such occasions. The judgment as to when, where and why confrontation is preferable than acquiescence, is an independent responsibility of the partners.

*Ninth, since the Civil War we have not known, and hope never to know, what national disaster other than the slavery issue could so tear the social fabric of the country apart as to disrupt the constitutional balance of the presidency and the Congress* beyond the point of no return. The constitution's survival after four assassinations of presidents, from Lincoln to Kennedy, and three bungled attempts, on Roosevelt, Truman and Reagan, tells us that no particular president is indispensable to the general order. What else?

Not by unemployment and economic despair, at any rate on the scale prevailing during the Pullman strike in Chicago in 1894; or in 1932 when the unemployment rate was 25% and President Hoover ordered the streets and parks of Washington cleared of bonus marchers by troops under the command of General Douglas MacArthur. And not by the demonstrations and unrest in 1968 and 1970, directed against the Vietnam war, when troops again were alerted.

It is pure speculation to suggest that a very different sort of civil-military encounter might, with the very best of wills on all sides, result in the suspension if not the doom of constitutional processes. Against the contingency of a full-scale war involving the major powers and the use or threat of nuclear weapons, elaborate preparations have been made to spirit the president, Congress and other high officials, on signal, away from Washington and into subterranean shelters tunneled under a mountain, designed on a scale spacious enough to accommodate living and the performance of official duties by those so sheltered. In such an environment access, communications and the like would almost necessarily be under the control, at least for some purposes and in moments of crisis, of military officers primarily concerned for the physical safety of the "inmates." It is difficult to conceive of elected officials, so sequestered from the people, conducting a government of separated and shared powers for any considerable length of time. It cannot be dismissed, alas, as inconceivable that such an event could occur before the 1980s are out. Constitutional government needs sunshine, not caves.

## TABLE I

*Pages of Public Law and Federal Register,*
*Selected Years*

| Years | Public Laws | Federal Register |
|-------|-------------|------------------|
| 1936 | 1,950 | 2,355 |
| 1946 | 1,088 | 14,736 |
| 1956 | 1,123 | 10,528 |
|  | 685* |  |
| 1964 | 1,111 | 19,304 |
| 1965 | 1,311 | 17,187 |
| 1966 | 1,600 | 16,850 |
| 1967 | 944 | 21,087 |
| 1968 | 1,361 | 20,068 |
| 1969 | 854 | 20,464 |
| 1970 | 2,080 | 20,032 |
| 1971 | 813 | 25,442 |
| 1972 | 1,517 | 28,920 |
| 1973 | 1,084 | 35,586 |
| 1974 | 2,359 | 45,422 |
| 1975 | 1,157 | 60,221 |
| 1976 | 2,960 | 57,072 |
| 1977 | 1,629 | 63,629 |
| 1978 | 3,778 | 61,261 |
| 1979 | 1,369 | 77,497 |
| 1980 | 3,582 | 86,667 |
| 1981 | 1,729 | 63,553 |

*Titles 10 and 32 U.S. Code enacted, adding to ordinary legislative output.

Source: Inspection of bound volumes of the *Federal Register, Statutes at Large,* and for years since 1976, *U.S. Code Congressional and Administrative News* (West Publishing Co.)

# APPENDIX

Participants in Miller Center-National Academy
of Public Administration Roundtable Series 1979–80 ·

John A. Armitage—University of Virginia
Christopher Arterton—Yale University
Richard Barrett—National Academy of Public
Dom Bonafede, Sr.—*The National Journal*
David S. Broder—*The Washington Post*
Richard A. Brody—Stanford University
McGeorge Bundy—New York University
Douglass Cater—Aspen Institute,
    formerly Special Assistant to President Johnson
The Honorable Richard B. Cheney—House of Representatives
Inis L. Claude—University of Virginia
James E. Connor—First Boston Corporation,
    formerly Cabinet Secretary to President Ford
Eric Davis—University of California at Berkeley
Alan Dean—National Academy of Public Administration
I. M. Destler—Carnegie Endowment for International Peace
The Honorable Hardy C. Dillard—Judge,
    International Court of Justice, 1970–1979
George Esser—National Academy of Public Administration
Richard F. Fenno, Jr.—University of Rochester
Louis Fisher—Congressional Research Service,
    Library of Congress
William T. R. Fox—Columbia University
Andrew J. Glass—Cox Newspapers
Ted Gest—*U.S. News and World Report*
Norman A. Graebner—University of Virginia
Wayne Granquist—Associate Director for Management
    and Regulatory Policy, Office of Management and Budget
Fred I. Greenstein—Princeton University
Erwin C. Hargrove—Vanderbilt University
John E. Harr—National Academy of Public Administration
Hugh Heclo—Harvard University
Phillip S. Hughes—National Academy of Public Administration

# Appendix

Dorothy B. James—Virginia Polytechnic Institute
and State University
Whittle Johnston—University of Virginia
Charles O. Jones—University of Pittsburgh
Anthony S. King—University of Essex,
American Enterprise Institute
Thomas E. Mann—American Political Science Association
Harvey C. Mansfield—Columbia University
Carl Marcy—American Committee on East-West Accord
The Honorable John O. Marsh—Counselor to the President,
1973–1974
Clifton H. McCleskey—University of Virginia
Frederick C. Mosher—University of Virginia
Hans J. Morgenthau—New School for Social Research
The Honorable Frank Moss—Schnader, Harrison, Segal
and Lewis, Washington, D.C.
Robert J. Myers—Council on Religion and International Affairs
(*The New Republic*, 1968–1979)
Michael Nacht—Harvard University
Anna Nelson—National Academy of Public Administration
Richard E. Neustadt—Harvard University
William C. Olson—The American University
Norman J. Ornstein—Center for Advanced Study
in Behavioral Science
E. Raymond Platig—Department of State
Nelson W. Polsby—University of California at Berkeley
Don K. Price—Harvard University
Donald Puchala—Columbia University
R. K. Ramazani—University of Virginia
Richard Rose—University of Strathclyde,
American Enterprise Institute
James H. Rowe—Corcoran, Youngman and Rowe
Lester Salamon—National Academy of Public Administration,
Urban Institute
Ray Scherer—RCA Corporation
Allen Schick—Congressional Research Service,
Library of Congress
Lester Seligman—University of Illinois,
American Enterprise Institute
Hedrick Smith—*The New York Times*

# Appendix

Elmer B. Staats—Comptroller General of the United States
Herbert Stein—University of Virginia
Sydney Stein, Jr.—National Academy of Public Administration
Donald C. Stone—Carnegie-Mellon University
James L. Sundquist—Brookings Institution
Peter Szanton—Hamilton, Rabinovitz and Szanton
Kenneth W. Thompson—White Burkett Miller Center of
    Public Affairs, University of Virginia
David B. Truman—President (emeritus), Mount Holyoke College
James Wall—*The Christian Century*
Kenneth N. Waltz—University of California at Berkeley
Warren Weaver—*The New York Times*
Harrison Wellford—Office of Management and Budget,
    Executive Associate Director for Reorganization
    and Management
The Honorable Charles Whalen—New Directions,
    Washington, D.C.
Murat Williams—Madison Mills, Virginia
Daniel Yankelovich—Yankelovich, Skelly and White, Inc.
James S. Young—White Burkett Miller Center of Public Affairs,
    University of Virginia
John D. Young—American University